WRITTEN IN WATER

WRITTEN IN WATER

the prose poems of
Luis Cernuda

Translated by Stephen Kessler

City Lights Books
San Francisco

Cover design and photo: Stephen Gutermuth/double-u-gee
Book design and typography: Harvest Graphics
Editor: Robert Sharrard

Grateful acknowledgment is due to the editors of the following magazines, where some of these translations first appeared: *Chelsea, Hawai'i Pacific Review, The Kenyon Review, Luna, New Orleans Review, Oxygen, Paragraph, Parnassus, Poetry International, The Redwood Coast Review, Sentence, Sulfur River Literary Review,* and *Two Lines.*

The late Cernuda scholar Alexander Coleman provided early impetus and advice for this project.

The translator also wishes to thank Ángel María Yanguas Cernuda for his generous encouragement and gracious hospitality in Seville.

And thanks are due as well to the National Endowment for the Arts for a fellowship, which helped to make the completion of this book possible.

Library of Congress Cataloging-in-Publication Data

Cernuda, Luis.
   [Prose poems. English]
   Written in water : the prose poems of Luis Cernuda : Ocnos and Variations on a Mexican theme / translated by Stephen Kessler.
     p.   cm.
   ISBN 0-87286-431-6
1. Cernuda, Luis—Translations into English. 2. Prose poems, Spanish—Translations into English. I. Kessler, Stephen, 1947- II. Cernuda, Luis. Ocnos. III. Cernuda, Luis. Variations on a Mexican theme.
   IV.   Title.
   PQ6605.E7A245 2004
   861'.62—dc22   2003025653

CONTENTS

TRANSLATOR'S PREFACE

One of the leading poets of Spain's prodigious Generation of 1927, Luis Cernuda may be less well known to English-language readers than such contemporaries as Federico García Lorca, Rafael Alberti, Pedro Salinas, Jorge Guillén, and Vicente Aleixandre. Like all of these, Cernuda was an Andalusian. Born in Seville in 1902, he was a student of Salinas at the university there, where he found his vocation and published his first poems before going abroad, at Salinas's suggestion, to teach for a year in Toulouse, France. Returning to Madrid in 1929, Cernuda encountered most of the other members of the gifted cohort that was transforming Spanish poetry. By the time the first edition of his collected poems, *La realidad y el deseo* (to be continually expanded throughout his career), was published in 1936 Cernuda's reputation was well established among his peers. But that was on the eve of the Civil War, and he left Spain in 1938 never to return.

First in England, then in Scotland, and eventually in the United States at Mount Holyoke College in Massachusetts, Cernuda earned his living as a literature professor but never felt at home in these northern latitudes. Triply marginalized as a poet, an exile, and a homosexual (writing openly about his sexuality long before it was morally or politically acceptable to be gay), he seems from his writings to have cultivated a sense of his own spiritual, intellectual, and esthetic aristocracy even as he finally chose the poverty of a life in Mexico where, from the early 1950s until his death of a heart attack in 1963, he found at least an echo or reflection of his youth in southern Spain. Though he returned to the U.S. briefly in the early 1960s to teach at

San Francisco State and UCLA, it was Mexico that claimed his soul with its language, its climate, and the warmth of its people.

While Cernuda's verse is vivid testimony to various aspects of this biographical itinerary, it is in his two books of prose poems, *Ocnos* and *Variaciones sobre tema mexicano*, that he traces more explicitly an outline of his life's journey. *Ocnos,* which takes its title from a figure in Roman myth symbolizing the fruitlessness of worldly labor, is a poetic autobiography in small scenes or vignettes beginning with his childhood in Seville and progressing through his lonely years in the States. Reviewing the first edition in 1943, Octavio Paz wrote: "In these memories and landscapes, in these notes toward the history of his sensibility, there is great objectivity: the poet doesn't set out to fantasize, or to lie to himself or anyone else. He attempts only to illuminate, with an almost impersonal light, something very personal: a few moments in his life. (But is it truly ours, this life we live?)"

The *Variations* chronicle, in somewhat more lyric form—due in part to the greater immediacy of the experiences being recorded—the restorative encounter with Mexico. Taken together, these two books offer a vivid portrait of the artist both as homeless wanderer and acute creative consciousness at work. Though published separately during his lifetime, Cernuda intended them as one book. With this edition we have them together in English for the first time.

In *Ocnos* especially we find an unusual combination of lyricism and analysis, subjective vision and objective description—as if the poetic truth of experience could be evoked only through the most rigorous observation and exact recollection combined with original sentiment and mature reflection. Cernuda's syntax is elaborate but only in the interest of greater precision in locating the emotional and philosophical essence of a given scene or moment. "Transparency, balance, objectivity, clarity of thought and word are the outward virtues of Cernuda's prose," notes Paz in his review. "Why speak of the deeper, more secret ones: the elegant simplicity, the melancholy with ironic traces, which never approaches satire and in which we perceive not so much the anger of an offended vanity as the tedium and weariness of a spirit without illusions."

In the Mexican variations, while similarly focused, one senses a more relaxed and immediate register of impressions and feelings as the writer enters a far more congenial environment than his years of exile have previously afforded him. It is the closest to a homecoming he can hope for during the seemingly endless years of the Franco dictatorship in Spain.

As the title of his collected poems, *Reality and Desire*, suggests, Cernuda's was a divided life, caught between the passion of erotic longing and the constraints of social convention—and later between the longing for home and the bitter fact of uprootedness. The title of this book is taken from a text not included in either *Ocnos* or the *Variations* but intended by the author as a kind of coda to both. It consciously echoes Keats's epitaph for himself: "Here lies one whose name was writ in water." A scholar of English literature who identified with Keats's tragic genius, Cernuda saw in his own predicament both a reflection of the English poet's brief career and a symbol of the human condition: mortal, ephemeral, doomed to disappear with scarcely a trace.

Up to now, the only substantial collection of Cernuda's verse available in English is Reginald Gibbons's translation of *Selected Poems* (originally published by

California in 1977, reissued in paperback in 2000 by Sheep Meadow Press). It is my hope that the prose poems, read alongside the verse, will begin to reveal the power and depth of the author's writing to readers unable to experience the Spanish directly. In this translation I've tried to respect the richness of the Cernuda's style while rendering it in an American English as musical, thoughtful, and speakable as the original.

STEPHEN KESSLER

OCNOS

It was as natural a thing for Ocnus to twist his reeds into rope as it was for the donkey to eat them. He could stop twisting them, but then what would he do with himself? That's why he prefers to twist the reeds, to give himself something to do; and that's why the donkey eats the rope, though if it weren't there he'd still have to eat it. It's possible that's how they'll learn something, or it will be more nourishing. And one might say, up to a point, that that's how Ocnus finds with his donkey a way to pass the time.

GOETHE

POETRY

On rare occasions our living room would take on a glow in late afternoon, and the sound of the piano filled the house, seizing me as I came to the foot of the echoing marble staircase, while the hazy shimmer of the light that gently flooded the upstairs hallway seemed to me an impalpable body, warm and golden, whose soul was music.

Was it music? Was it the unusual? Both sensations, that of the music and of the unusual, came together leaving a mark on me, in me, that time has never managed to erase. I glimpsed then the existence of a different reality from the one perceived every day, and now I sensed obscurely how being different wasn't enough for that other reality, but that something winged and sacred should come with it and give it a kind of halo, like the trembling nimbus surrounding a point of light.

And so, in the unconscious dream of a child's soul, there now appeared the magical power that offers consolation, and ever since then that's how I see it floating before my eyes: like that hazy radiance I once witnessed sketching itself through darkness, gently rustling with its shimmering wing the pure and crystalline notes of melody.

NATURE

The child took pleasure in following patiently, day after day, the mysterious sprouting of plants and their flowers. The appearance of a leaf, its translucent green still folded and scarcely visible next to the stem where yesterday it wasn't there, filled him with astonishment, and with attentive eyes, for hours at a time, he loved catching its movement, its invisible growing, the way others love to catch, in flight, the flapping wings of a bird.

To take a tender cutting from a mature plant and root it apart, with a touch he wished to be soft and smooth as air, the care it then required, keeping it shaded the first days, watering its thirst each morning and evening when the weather was warm, absorbed him in a selfless expectation.

What joy when he saw the leaves break out at last, and their tender color, which in their transparency seemed luminous, revealing in relief the veins, darkening little by little with the stronger sap. He felt as if he himself had worked the miracle of giving life, of awakening out of the basic earth, like a god, the form until then asleep in the dream of nonexistence.

AUTUMN

Enchantment of the autumns of your childhood, seduction of a time of year that is yours, because that's when you were born.

The atmosphere of summer, thick until then, lightened and took on a sharpness through which sounds were almost painful, piercing your flesh like a rose's thorn. The first rains fell around mid-September, announced by thunder and the sky suddenly clouding over, with a steely pounding of waters unleashed against the prison of windows. Your mother's voice said: "Lower the awning," and behind that sharp complaint (like that of the swallows crisscrossing the blue sky over the patio) which raised the canvas to fold it over the wires that held it up, the rain poured into the house, lightly moving its silvery feet with a rhythmic sound on the marble floor.

From the wet leaves, from the damp earth, a delicious aroma rose, and the rainwater gathered in the hollow of your hand had a taste of that smell, akin to the essence of its origin, dark and penetrating, like that of a crumpled magnolia blossom. It seemed to be returning to some sweet custom from a strange and far-off place. And at night, in bed, you shrank your body, feeling how young and pure and light it was, around your soul, made one with it, become your soul itself.

THE PIANO

Next door to your house lived the family of that pianist, who was always away in distant lands, in cities around whose names your imagination placed a magical halo, and who sometimes returned for a few weeks to his own country and family. Though it wasn't by seeing him come down the street, with his vaguely foreign and very artistic air, that you knew he was back, as night fell the piano told you.

Along the hallways you went toward the room on the other side of whose wall he was practicing, and all alone there in the dark, deeply enchanted without knowing why, you listened to those languid phrases, so penetratingly melancholy, which called and spoke to your child's soul, evoking a past and a future equally unknown.

Years later you heard those same sounds again, recognizing them and attributing them now to that musician you so loved, yet the immensity, the expectation of a latent elemental force awaiting some supreme expression seemed still to go on existing in them beneath the fame of their author, a force which, given form, must break out into the light.

A child pays attention not to names but events, and in these to the power that drives them. What in the solitary shadows of a room drew you to the wall, and left you longing and nostalgic when the piano fell silent, was music itself, before and beyond whoever discovers and interprets it, like the springs of which rivers and even the sea are only the tangible and finite forms.

ETERNITY

As a child he possessed a blind religious faith. He wanted to do good works, not because he expected reward or feared punishment, but out of the instinct for following a beautiful order established by God, in which the irruption of evil was as much a matter of dissonance as of sin. But into this childish notion of God was mixed insidiously that of eternity. And sometimes in bed, awake earlier than usual, in the early morning silence of the house, he was assaulted by fear of eternity, of time without end.

The word forever, applied to the consciousness of the spiritual being inside him, filled him with terror, which then became lost in a sense of dissolution, like a drowning body vanishing in waves of an oceanic flood. He felt his life attacked by two enemies, one in front of him and one behind, not wanting to go forward yet unable to turn back. This, if it had been possible, is what he would have preferred: to go back, return to that hazy unremembered region from which he had first come into the world.

From what mysterious depth in him did those thoughts spring? He tried to force his memory, to recover the consciousness of where, calm and unconscious, amid clouds of unknowing, he had been taken by God's hand and pulled into time and life. Sleep was again the only thing that answered his questions. And then that voiceless, unconsoling response was incomprehensible.

THE NURSERY

Sometimes we'd go out to buy a fan palm or a rosebush for the patio. Since the nursery was some distance away we'd have to take the carriage; and on arriving I could make out through the gate the paths of dark earth, the little walkways bordered with geraniums, the big jasmine vine covering one of the whitewashed walls.

Francisco the nurseryman, followed by his wife, would greet us with smiles. They had no children, and they tended their nursery and spoke of it as if it were a baby. At times they'd even lower their voices and point to an ailing plant, so it wouldn't hear, poor thing, how much it worried them.

At the back of the nursery was the greenhouse, a gallery of frosted glass with a little green door at one end. Inside, there was a warm, dark smell that went to my head: the smell of damp earth mixed with the leaves' perfume. My skin felt rubbed by the air pressing against me, dense and moist. Here grew the palms, the banana trees, the ferns, and at their feet the orchids appeared, with their petals like iridescent scales, an impossible cross between flower and snake.

The pressure of the air would slowly turn to an intimate unease, and I imagined with alarm and delight that among the leaves, in some solitary corner of the greenhouse, was hidden a lovely baby, different from the other ones I knew, and that soon and for my eyes alone it was going to reveal itself.

Was it that belief which invested that place with such enchantment? Now I think I can understand what I couldn't have known then: how that enclosed space of the greenhouse, that marshy, mysterious atmosphere where invisible babies may have been hiding, was for me the perfect image of an Eden, suggested by smell, by shade and water, as in Góngora's line: "Green street, sweet light, cold window."

FEAR

for Guadalupe Dueñas

Along the solitary country road, its edges dotted with prickly pear and the occasional eucalyptus, in the rhythm of the mule-drawn carriage, the child was riding back to the city from that village with the Arabic name. How old would he have been then—five, six? He himself didn't know, because time, the idea of time had yet to enter his soul. But that nightfall would fill it with another new and terrible idea, which only an adult is able to face, if he ever can.

Through the carriage window he could see the sky losing its color, from the intense blue of the afternoon to the faded azure of twilight, and from there slowly filling with shadow. Would night overtake him far from home outside the city—night from whose darkness he'd been protected up to then by the friendly walls, the lit lamp shining on the picture book?

A fear, whose sudden appearance he may not have been fully aware of, noticing the effect more than its cause, warned him against the nocturnal world of the open countryside—fear in the face of the strange and the unfamiliar, which began to translate in his child's consciousness, quickly, anxiously, dreadfully, into the pressure of relentless motion (as the mules of the carriage picked up their pace) fleeing ahead.

Many years later he'd tell you that he himself didn't recognize that voice rising from deep inside, dark and afraid, saying, "Night is falling, night is falling," as a way of warning the others, who hadn't noticed, who perhaps were powerless against that previously unknown horror: the horror of powers loose in the world and set against men and waiting to ambush life.

You, who knew him well, can relate (with the inevitable margin of error there is between the deep and incorruptible center of a human being and the external perception of another, however close a friend) that awakening of a primal and ancestral terror in a soul predestined to feel it forever, even if intermittently, to the expression he himself, when he was a man, would later give it in a line of poetry: "For fear of traveling all alone into the shadow of time."

THE BAZAAR

In the dim light beveled moons of mirrors and crystals shone, and the blended smells of perfume and Russian leather floated in the air. Behind the glass and the shop-windows, against the dark velvet of the cases, glimmering iridescent reflections of silver and porcelain as in the lining of a sea shell, stood big bottles of cologne or the more delicate flasks of perfume. There was barely space left for the pieces of *modern style* furniture, whose irregular and surprising shapes stood out here and there among the pure and vivid colors of the toys. It was a rich and varied mixture of colors, smells and reflections.

The enchantment of that atmosphere was made all the more mysterious by long thin rectangular tags, where the name of the bazaar appeared in white relief against a scarlet background, and which stood out against the cardboard of the boxes that for my saint's day or Christmas brought home to me marvelous toys, wrapped in silky paper and curly wisps of wood shavings like locks of blond hair.

The bazaar's atmosphere was a feminine atmosphere, and its special seduction didn't disperse with the objects that left there, in little packages tied with a ribbon, hidden in the huge sleeve of a woman. And even though, with a light rustle of silk, the toes of her shoes barely poking out from under her long skirt, she would go down the marble stairs to settle in the carriage waiting outside, that enchantment didn't disappear. It remained floating, impersonal and indivisible, like the aroma of leather, rice powder and Hercules allheal, now a history, a legend and an age unto itself.

TIME

There comes a moment in life when time catches up with us. (I'm not sure how well I'm expressing this.) I mean that from a certain age we see ourselves subject to time and obliged to take it into account, as if some angry vision with a flaming sword had hurled us from the first paradise, where everyone at one time lived free from the sting of death. Those childhood years when time doesn't exist! A day, a few hours then are an eternity. How many centuries fit inside the hours of a child?

I remember that corner of the patio in the house where I was born, all by myself and sitting on the bottom step of the marble staircase. The awning was down, casting a cool shadow over the atmosphere, and on the canvas, through which the noonday light came streaming, softly filtered, a star stuck out its six points of red fabric. In the opening of the patio the wide leaves of the fan palms, a dark and shiny green, reached up to the open balconies, and below, around the fountain, the flowering shrubs and oleanders and azaleas were gathered. The falling water sounded with a steady, lulling rhythm, and there under the water a few red goldfish swam in a darting motion, their scales shimmering like gold lightning. Dissolved in that atmosphere was a languor that slowly came to invade my entire body.

There, in the absolute silence of summer, underscored by the murmuring water, my eyes open to the clear half-darkness that heightens the mysterious life of things, I saw how time can hold still, suspended in air, like the cloud that conceals a god, pure and weightless, never passing.

STREET CRIES

They were three street cries.

One when spring had come, late in the afternoon, the balconies open, and floating up to them on the breeze a sharp aroma, rough and hard, that almost tickled your nose. People went by: women dressed in light, sheer fabrics; men, some in black wool or yellowish suits, and others in discolored white linen jackets and carrying wicker lunch trays, empty, on their way home from work. Then, a few streets over, the cry went up—"Carnations! Carnations!"— a slightly muffled cry, whose sound that sharp aroma, that same rough, scratchy scent that rose on the breeze to the opened balconies, converged with and merged in the scent of carnations. Dissolved in the air it had floated nameless, bathing the afternoon, until the cry betrayed it, giving it a voice and a sound, plunging it deep in your chest, like a knife whose scar time will never heal.

The second street cry was at noon, in summer. The awning was unfurled over the patio, keeping the house cool and shady. The door to the street scarcely allowed an echo of light to penetrate the entryway. Water sounded in the drowsy fountain under its corona of green leaves. What a pleasure it was in the laziness of the summer noon, in that sleepy atmosphere, to rock in the wicker rocker. Everything was light, afloat; the world turned slowly, like a soap bubble, delicate, iridescent, unreal. And suddenly, from outside the doors, from the street flooded with sunlight, came the wild cry, like a moan of pleasure, "Mackerel!" The same as when you're stirred from sleep in the middle of the night and that vague awakening brings with it just enough awareness that you can feel the surrounding calm and quiet, and you turn and fall back to sleep. There was in that cry a sudden bolt of gold and scarlet light, like lightning flashing through the darkness of an aquarium, that sent a sudden chill through your flesh. The world, having stopped for a moment, resumed its smooth turning, turning.

The third cry was at nightfall, in autumn. The lamplighter had already passed, with his long hook on his shoulder, at whose far end flickered the little blue flame like a soul, lighting the streetlamps. The paving stones, damp from the first rains, shone under the bluish gas light. A balcony here, a door there, began to be lit up along the opposite wall, so close together in the narrow street. Then you could hear the blinds being lowered, the shutters closing. Through the balcony's sheer curtain, his forehead pressed against the cold window, the little boy watched the street for a moment, waiting. Then came the voice of the old peddler, filling the dusk with his hoarse cry, "Fresh lavender!"—the vowels closed in on themselves like the ululating call of an owl. He could be guessed at more than seen, dragging one foot behind him, stormcloud face beneath the hat brim fallen on him like a roof tile, moving, with his sack of lavender over his shoulder, to close the cycle of the year and of life itself.

The first cry was the voice, the pure voice; the second the song, the melody; the third the memory and the echo, voice and melody now vanished.

THE POET AND THE MYTHS

Quite early in life, before you'd ever read a poem, a book of mythology fell into your hands. Those pages revealed to you a world where poetry, like flame bringing firewood to life, transformed what was real. How sad your own religion seemed to you then. You didn't discuss this, nor did you doubt, a difficult thing for a child; but in your most deeply rooted beliefs was insinuated, if not a rational objection, the presentiment of some absent joy. Why did they teach you to bow your head before sacred suffering, when in another time men were happy enough to worship beauty in all its tragic plenitude?

It hardly matters that you couldn't have understood then the profound connection between certain myths and certain timeless forms of life. Any aspiration there may be in you toward poetry, those Greek myths were what provoked and guided you—though you had no one at your side to warn you of the risk you were running as you steered your life instinctively in accord with a reality invisible to most people, and toward nostalgia for a spiritual and physical harmony broken and exiled centuries since from among the living.

SCANDAL

In the long summer evenings, the entryways washed down, the jasmine seller past, they would appear, alone at times, more often in pairs. They'd be dressed in starched white jackets, tight black wool slacks, shoes that squeaked like crickets, and wearing little tilted caps from which a curl of blond or black hair might flare. They slinked along with the grace of cats, proud of something only they understood, seeming to keep it a secret, though the pleasure they found in this secret spilled over in spite of themselves onto others.

A chorus of falsetto shrieks, the barking of a dog, announced them even before they had turned the corner. Finally they appeared, laughing and almost conceited at the cortege that followed behind them spewing insults and calling them names. With the dignity of lofty personages in exile, they scarcely even turned to their cursing entourage to fire off some witty retort. But as if not wanting to disappoint people in what they expected, they swung their hips more dramatically, pulling their jackets tighter to their swaying shapes, which provoked even louder and ruder jokes from the chorus.

Sometimes they'd look up to a balcony, where the curious stuck their heads out at the noise, and in their brazen youthful eyes shone an even greater mockery, a more authentic contempt than that of the sick busybodies pestering them. Finally they disappeared at the far end of the street.

They were the mysterious creatures known as "fairies."

SUMMER MORNINGS

On some religious holidays whose celebration had an especially local or familiar resonance, festivals that always happened in summer, the boy went out in the morning, headed for church. Sometimes they took him to the cathedral, sometimes farther, to some working-class neighborhood rarely or never visited, where the church in question was, and on occasion he even had to cross the river, whose dense green brilliance resembled molten metal flowing between the clay-colored banks.

Everything happened in such an unusual atmosphere. In the first place it was the going and coming back home in hours when the heat was already bearing down, because most summer outings normally happened in late afternoon or evening. Then it was the moving though the morning streets, some shaded with awnings, others wide open to the sunshine in a way he would never again encounter anywhere else. And finally it was to view up close in passing the calm activity of the bustling neighborhood and the market.

The forms and colors in that atmosphere had so much grace, softened somehow and a little hazy, their hardness or shrillness muted. Here was the fruit stand (figs, apricots, plums), over which reigned the dark green roundness of the watermelon, sometimes cut open to reveal inside its cool red and white freshness. Or the pottery stand (vases, sculptures, bottles), with the rounded bellies of bowls or throats of vessels in pink or orange tones. Or the candy displays (dates, pastries, cream-filled bon-bons, nougats), which exuded a sweet and almondy smell with a whiff of Eastern dew.

But always above all that—the color, the movement, the heat, the brilliance—floated an air so clean that it seemed as yet unbreathed by anyone else, bringing with it also something of that same sensation of the unusual, of surprise, that stunned the boy's soul and awakened in him a muffled, deep and selfless pleasure. A pleasure that later those of the intellect, or even those of sex, could never equal in their hold on his memory.

It seemed as if his senses, and through them his body, were a poised and fine-tuned instrument for the world to strum its seldom-heard melody. But to the boy it didn't feel strange at all, even though it was rare, that precious gift of feeling completely attuned with life and brimming with it, transformed and carried away. He was drunk on life and he didn't know it; he was alive as few are, as only a poet can be and understand.

VICE

On the way to school, along that street of stately houses beyond whose gates one could glimpse the big patios, and amid the white marble one slender green solitary palm tree, a certain house whose blinds were always down and whose entrance was always shut behind a heavy door, mysterious as a convent, fascinated me. What kind of family, what hidden community, could live there? Not once, in my daily comings and goings past it, did I see an open balcony, and only rarely the greengrocer stopping his donkey to hand through the iron gate, its shutters barely opened, his fresh and gleaming merchandise of tomatoes, cucumbers and lettuces.

One winter morning, headed for school a bit early, making my way through the dawn's dimness, crossing that street I saw a carriage parked in front of the house, the electric light still glowing red in one window; a taxi, old and battered, with its top down, and the driver with a white bandanna tied around his neck, an oilcloth cap tilted on his head and his legs crossed casually, like someone waiting. Along the sidewalk, a tall woman dressed in yellow, fur coat draped over one shoulder, was walking past yelling angrily next to the front door of the house, which for once was open.

Some childish fear prevented me from going anywhere near her, and from the opposite sidewalk I could see her pale, dull face, heavily caked with makeup, coarse bleached hair with dark roots along the part above her forehead, which was both scary and ridiculous, something like that of a limp doll losing its stuffing. Through the open iron gate of the house came a mist of stale perfume, of depravity overlooked by the law and ignored by religion. The coachman, perched on his bench, was laughing at the woman's tirade, and leaning awkwardly against the door jamb, drowsy and bemused, a policeman watched her.

HIDDEN BEAUTY

Albanio was crossing the threshold of adolescence and was about to leave the house where he had been born and had lived until then, for another on the outskirts of the city. It was a mild and luminous March afternoon, suffused with the look and feel and smell of early spring in that nearly uninhabited landscape.

He was standing in the empty room that was to be his in the new house, and through the open window the breeze was blowing the pure young aroma of the countryside, brightening the flame of the green and golden light, increasing the power of the afternoon. Leaning against the window frame, nostalgic without knowing what for, he gazed at the landscape a long while.

In a kind of intuition more than perception, for the first time in his life he sensed the beauty of everything his eyes beheld. And with the vision of that hidden beauty a feeling of solitude he'd never known before slipped into him like something stabbing his soul.

The weight of the treasure nature was entrusting to him was too much for his lonely, still childish spirit, for that richness seemed to infuse him with a responsibility, a duty, and he felt the need to lighten the burden by communicating it to others. But then a strange shyness overcame him, sealing his lips, as if the price of that gift were the melancholy and isolation that came with it, condemning him to enjoy and suffer in silence the bitter and divine drunkenness, incommunicable and ineffable, that flooded his heart and clouded his eyes with tears.

THE CATHEDRAL AND THE RIVER

To go in late afternoon to the cathedral, when the great harmonious nave, vaulted and resonant, was dozing off with its arms spread out in a cross. Between the main altar and the choir, a carpet of deaf red velvet absorbed the sound of footsteps. Everything was submerged in half-darkness, although light, still filtering through the stained glass, left its warm halo floating high up in the air. Tumbling from the dome like a waterfall, the great reliefs were just a tumult of gold shapes lost in shadow. And behind the railings, out of a canvas dark as a dream, emerged white hooded forms, ecstatic and charged with energy.

Then the organ took up its hazy prelude, slowly expanding its melody until the naves were filled with powerful voices, resounding with the dominion of the trumpets that will call up the souls on Judgment Day. But then it grew gentle again, laying down its power like a sword, and breathed lovingly, resting above the abyss of its fury.

Through the choir ever so silently, crossing the nave till they reached the steps of the main altar, the priests advanced under the weight of their vestments, preceded by the acolytes, boys with Murillo faces, dressed in red and white, carrying lit candlesticks. And behind them walked the choir boys, in their blue and silver robes, holding their feathered caps, which once they reached the altar, they placed on their heads, then took a few dance steps, between a *seguidilla* and a minuet, while the castanets clicked lightly in their little hands.

*

To go in late afternoon along the river of calm and luminous water, while the sun was starting to set amid purplish wisps of cirrus bordering the pure line of the horizon. Farther upstream, beyond the beautifully classical white facade of La Caridad, thick walls hid the train station, the smoke, the noise, the fever of men. Then, in solitude again, the river was as green and mysterious as a mirror, reflecting the vast sky, the flowering acacias, the clay-colored slope of the shoreline.

Some youthful laughs disturbed the silence, and there on the opposite bank a flash split the air followed by a splash in the water. Naked among the tree trunks along the bank, their bodies agile with a shimmer of green bronze barely darkened by the soft down of puberty, some boys were swimming.

You could hear the whistle of a train, the chirping of a flight of swallows; then silence again. Light was slowly going out of the sky, yet the color lingered, turning a clear turquoise. And the ironic croaking of the frogs started up on cue, to cut short the exaltation raised in your soul by the calm of the place, the grace of youth and the beauty of the hour.

ANCIENT GARDEN

First you went down a long dark corridor. At the end, through an archway, the garden's light appeared, a light whose golden glow tinged the leaves and the water in a pond with green. And the pond, as you came out into the light, enclosed behind an iron railing, glimmered like an emerald liquid, dense, calm and mysterious.

Then there was the stairway, beside whose steps grew two tall magnolias, concealing among their branches an old statue atop a column that served as a pedestal. At the foot of the stairway the garden's terraces began.

Following the paths of rose-colored bricks, through a wrought-iron gate and down some steps, there was a series of little solitary patios, with myrtles and oleanders around a mossy fountain, and next to the fountain the trunk of a cypress whose crown was immersed in the luminous air.

In the surrounding silence, all that beauty throbbed with a hidden pulse, as if the hearts of all the vanished people who had once enjoyed the garden were beating concealed behind the thick branches. The sound of flowing water was like their footsteps running away.

The sky was a pure and limpid blue, resplendent with light and heat. Among the tops of the palms, beyond the roofs and white galleries crowning the garden, one gray and ochre tower stood slim and erect like the calyx of a flower.

*

There are human destinies that are linked to a place or a landscape. There in that garden, sitting at the edge of a fountain, you once dreamed of life as inexhaustible enchantment. The sky's immensity spurred you to action; the breath of the flowers, the leaves, the water, to give yourself to pleasure without remorse.

Later you came to understand that neither action nor pleasure could be lived with the perfection they had in your dreams beside the fountain. And the day you understood this sad truth, though you were far away in a foreign land, you longed to return to that garden and sit down again on the edge of that fountain, to dream once more of your lost youth.

THE POET

Albanio would still be very small when he read Bécquer for the first time. They were some volumes bound in blue with gold arabesques, and in between the yellowing pages someone had slipped some photographs of old cathedrals and ruined castles. They had been given to Albanio's sisters by their cousins, because in those days there was a lot of vague talk about Bécquer, whose remains were being taken to Madrid for a magnificent burial in the university chapel.

Among the most densely printed pages of prose, as he leafed through those books, he found other, airier pages, with short lines in light rhythms. He didn't grasp then (though not because he was a child, since most grown men don't grasp this either) the unhappy human story rescued by the pure words of a poet. Yet reading without comprehending, like a child and like many men, he was infected with something different and mysterious, which later, on rereading the poet again and again, awakened in him something like the memory of an earlier life, vague and insistent, drowned in neglect and nostalgia.

Years later, now clearly capable, in his own unhappiness, of admiration, of love and of poetry, Albanio often entered the university chapel, stopping in one corner, where under a stone canopy an angel holds a book in one hand while raising the other to its lips, one finger held there, imposing silence. Although he knew that Bécquer wasn't there, but below, in the crypt of the chapel, alone, as the dead and the living always find themselves, Albanio gazed at that image a long time, as if its silent eloquence were not enough to make heard, awake in sound, the message of those stony lips. And the ones who answered his questioning were the young voices, the living laughter of the students, which through the thick walls reached him from the sunny courtyard. There inside, everything was now indifference and oblivion.

PLEASURE

On spring nights, late, with dawn approaching, across the fields, from Eritaña, came the sound of a hand organ. The ephemeral tune, in the calm and quiet of the night, took on a voice and spoke of those who at that hour, instead of sleeping, were living, staying awake for the pleasure of a moment. I would see them, men and women, a little tipsy but serious, their gazes intent and vague at the same time, holding onto each other as if moving to the rhythm of a spasm more than a dance, their hands wildly caressing the beautiful human body, triumphant for a day if only to be plunged later into death. And the hoarse, sharp cry of some peacock, sleepless among the poplars in the park, broke through the cadence of the tune like a joke at the expense of my crazy, sad desire.

I was just a boy, my desire was unformed, and the fervor stirring it had no focus; and I could only think enviously of those anonymous people having such fun at that hour, maybe a little coarsely, but they were superior to me because they knew pleasure, for which I had only a longing. And I asked myself if they were worthy of that knowledge, if I would be worthy to have it someday, just like any other perfect creature of animal grace, barely glimpsed by me at the bend of some street, whose sudden memory later flashed in my consciousness.

Through the flowering acacia branches, on the mild air of the May night, from the garden of the inn, the high thin sound of the music persisted. It wasn't the voice of some immortal melody, which persuades us that we, like it, will go on this way forever; it was fragile and perishable and it spoke of our doubt, urging us to enjoy ourselves, with an accent turned dramatic by the night and the occasion, like a voice from behind some ridiculous mask—grave, deep, passionate—warning us.

THE MAGNOLIA

You entered the street through an archway. It was narrow, so narrow you could walk down the middle and, extending your arms, touch the wall on either side. Then, through an iron gate, it went off at an angle into a labyrinth of other alleyways and little plazas that made up that old part of town. At the end of the street there was just one little door that was always shut, and it seemed as if the only way through were over the tops of the houses, up into the dazzling blue sky.

At a bend in the street was the balcony, which you could climb to, almost effortlessly, from the ground; and beside it, above the thick walls of the garden, the huge magnolia erupted covering everything with its branches. Among the sharp and shiny leaves were perched, in springtime, with that subtle mystery of the unspoiled, the snow-white flakes of its flowers.

That magnolia was always for me something more than a gorgeous reality: in it was encoded the image of life itself. Although at times I might want it some other way, more free, more in the stream of people and things, I knew it was precisely that separate life of the tree, that flowering without witnesses, that gave its beauty such a special quality. It was consumed in its own ardor, and in its solitude it put out such pure flowers, like a sacrifice rejected at the altar of a god.

THE CITY FROM A DISTANCE

In the splendor of a summer noon the boat was headed downriver toward San Juan. Along the riverbanks cicadas sang among the poplar and chestnut branches, and the water, a cloudy clay-pink color, folded lazily back over the iridescent wake. In the heavy heat of the air, the way the water gently rocked the boat felt good, carrying us lightly along, bodies without desire, souls without a care.

The village was on the slope of a little hill. The white houses, the green railings, were below, and along the trail going up, its steepness eased by steps and leveled landings, the dust gleamed beneath the silvery shadow of the olive trees.

Above was the church, and inside it, in back, on the other side of the darkness, you could glimpse the garden: a gallery covered with a green bower that the light tinged with a shimmering golden glow. As you went outside, onto the slope of the terrace, the expanse of lowland appeared, the earth whose warm tones obscured the planted fields, the broad calm river where sunlight sparkled on the water.

Beyond that, on the far side, was the city, the airy silhouette of its sharp-edged buildings, which the light, veiling them in the distance, cast in a silver-gray tone. Above all the houses stood the cathedral, and above that the tower, slender as a tawny palm. At the foot of the city the river sprouted rigging, the masts and ropes and sails of the anchored boats.

Next to the whitewashed wall where that balcony opened, on the terrace, was placed a bench that offered a seat in the shade. Everything appeared spread out below: farmland, river, city, all gently stirring like a body in sleep.

And the sound of the cathedral bells, arriving pure and weightless across the air, was like the very breathing of its dream.

THE TEACHER

I had him for a class in rhetoric, and he was short, chubby, with glasses like the ones Schubert wears in his portraits, walking through the cloisters in small slow strides, breviary in hand or with his hands resting in his cloak pockets, cap pushed well back on his large head with its thick gray hair. Nearly always quiet, or when paired with another professor speaking in measured tones, his voice strong and resonant, but most of the time alone in his cell, where he kept a few secular books mixed in with the religious ones, and from which I could see in springtime the green leaves and dark fruit of a mulberry tree climbing the wall and covering the gloomy little patio his window opened on.

One day in class he tried to read us some verses, his voice aglow with heartfelt enthusiasm, and it must have been hard for him to understand the mockery, veiled at first, then open and hostile, of the students—because he admired poetry and its art, in a pedantic way, naturally. It was he who tried to get me to recite sometimes, although a shyness stronger than pleasure froze my delivery; he who encouraged me to write my first poems, critiquing them then and giving me as an esthetic precept what in my literary papers would always be a graceful hold on the material.

He put me at the head of the class, a distinction for which I soon paid with a certain unpopularity among my schoolmates, and before final exams, as if understanding my diffidence and lack of confidence, he told me: "Go to the chapel and pray. That will give you courage."

Once I got to the university, in my self-absorption I stopped going to see him. One deep gold morning in fall, on my way to my early first class, I saw a poor little funeral turn-

ing the corner, the red brick wall of the school, which I'd for-
gotten; it was his. It was my heart, without hearing from any-
one else, that told me so. He must have died alone. I don't
know how he held up through those last days of his life.

THE FLOOD

November and February are months of torrential rains there. On the streets near the river they prepared the houses against flooding, reinforcing doorways with big planks. But in a neighborhood on the other side a stream also used to overflow with the rains, and its waters would spread out, smooth as a mirror in love with its own reflection, over the plain where the city lay.

One morning they came to get him at school at an unusual hour. It had been raining, day after day, torrentially; and with the water already flooding the fields, it would be hard for him to get back home in the outskirts if he delayed much longer. They had to leave the carriage in order to get through the last streets. That avenue of chestnut trees he had walked so often, now you needed a boat to get across.

The water covered everything, and in the deepest places strange buildings with straight lines sprang up out of the lagoon behind a delicate row of trees. A few people wandered confused and helpless over bridges that had just been built out of boards. But houses and people now seemed brief and transient, as if the water by depriving them of their usual earthly base (this happens to a ship when it puts out to sea) had given that truth its real scope and significance.

And at home, behind a balcony window, he looked down at the garden, which a wall protected from the water. The lagoon, with its fragile little bridges, black lines without perspective under a flat gray sky streaked with white by the rain, was like the landscape on a Japanese fan that belonged to his mother.

When night fell, with the electrical posts and lines blown down by the storm, there was no light. By candle-light, a book held before his sleepy eyes, he listened to the wind outside, in the flooded land, and the driving rain falling hour after hour. It felt like he was on an island, separate from the world and its boring tasks on an endless vacation; an island rocked by waters singing a lullaby to the last dreams of his childhood.

THE JOURNEY

On the shelves of his father's library, and hidden, because he wasn't allowed to use them, the boy found some volumes bound in red and gold, whose illustrated pages cast a deep and unspeakably engrossing spell. Those bindings were perhaps what first caught his attention, more than the names of the unknown cities printed on their spines: Rome, Paris, Berlin. Later, in other corners of the library and not so visible, he found unbound sheets of the same kinds of books; but this time the countries and the regions they spoke of were more remote: India, Japan, vast territories of the African and American continents. Then he discovered that some of those works were famous in the literature of travel, like that of Captain Cook or Stanley's explorations in search of Livingstone. The boy at that time knew only how to pore over the engravings at great length and go from them to the text, soaking up the variousness, the vastness, the marvelousness of the world.

The desire to see those actual cities, those countries the books spoke of hadn't yet awakened in him. He was so happy, so utterly happy leafing through and reading his books: imagination was enough, that interior vision, whose richness inside him he didn't understand, even though it was in his possession. And with his big book under the lamp in winter or sitting on one of the steps (the coolness of the marble was another inducement to summer reading) of the stairs going down to the patio, in the sweet light filtered through the awning, he read and read, looked and looked, treasuring in his mind rivers and oceans, landscapes and cities, streets and squares, buildings and monuments. (So well that, years later, on his first visit to one of those cities in his books, he would recognize it all as if he had lived there in a previous existence.)

But with those and other readings he came to learn that neither life nor the world were, or at least weren't only, that familiar corner, those walls that stood watch over his childhood; and so the seed of his adolescent curiosity was planted, the germ of a terrible ache (terrible in the case, which was precisely his, of one who, deprived of fortune, might settle in one place and spend his whole life there, earning in some thankless job just enough to get from one day to the next): the ache made up of a desire to see the world, to look at whatever we fancy as necessary, or simply pleasing, for the formation or satisfaction of our spirit.

And little by little, this ailment aggravated by the crisis of growing into adolescence, the horn of a ship in port or a train whistle in the countryside stabbed him like a dagger, goading his imagination always ready for a voyage. And much more if you believe, as he did, that what our desire fails to find close by is bound to be found far off. Someone said it long ago: he who travels across the sea changes skies but not his heart—which might well be true (though not in this particular case we're speaking of), but we'll never know that our heart won't change unless we cross the seas. Which in itself is reason enough to go from one place to another, and so at least sustain, alive and awake however late, the soul's curiosity, and its youth.

THE SMITTEN

You were at the summer theater, where night and the stars were what those gathered creatures saw overhead, nullifying with a mystery more real, an immensity more dramatic, the trivial happenings onstage. Sitting among his own crowd, like you among yours, not far from you he appeared, provoking with his presence, from the depths of your being, that inescapable attraction, both happy and painful, by which one person, feeling more himself than ever, ceases at the same time to belong to himself.

A strange shyness, perhaps the defense of someone at risk of being swept away, drew you inward, while an instinctive sympathy threw you outward, toward that being with whom you didn't know how much you longed to be entangled. Enlivened by dark eyes, crowned with long straight hair, that face enchanted you, poised atop a neck like a stem, with a graceful and unconscious sense of its own beauty.

It wasn't the first time you'd been smitten, although it was perhaps the first time that feeling, still unnamed, imposed itself on your consciousness. Then you'd forgotten the feeling, far from its source, as one forgets a brief awakening at dawn when daylight is barely breaking and the body falls back into the ignorance of sleep. Nor did you think it possible that you'd never see him again, unnoticed in the urgency of time, so early still, which scarcely if ever in life affords us space for the tenderness of which we might be capable.

*

That night struck inside you just a spark of the fire in which you'd later be consumed, only to rise like a phoenix. But in its flash you glimpsed the young body's beauty, almost without yet knowing enough to desire it, which no flower equals in color, in contour, in grace, being or seeming to be, besides, capable of responding to the passionate admiration of a lover.

Others may speak of how physical beauty withers and decays, but you desire only to remember its first splendor, and despite its melancholy ending, that shining moment will never be obscured. Some believe beauty, in its very being, is eternal *(Como dal fuoco il caldo, esser diviso—Non può'l bel dall'eterno),* and even when it isn't, it's like a calm in a current fed by the same flowing water, a pool whose contemplation is the only thing that seems to lift us beyond time for the duration of one uncontainable instant.

EVENING

In the long summer evenings we went up to the terrace. On the moss-covered bricks, between the railings and the whitewashed walls, there in the corner, was the jasmine bush, its dark branches covered with little white corollas, next to the moonflower vine, which at that hour was opening its little blue bells.

The setting sun tinged the borders of a few delicate white clouds resting along the horizon of rooftops with touches of gold and crimson. The panorama of arches, galleries and terraces seemed to keep shifting its profile: a white labyrinth stained here or there with pure colors, where at times a clothesline floated, its hanging wash billowing in the breeze with a seagoing air.

Gradually the bowl of the sky filled with a dark blue where the stars would swarm like snowflakes. Leaning on the rail, it felt good to be caressed by the wind. And the perfume of the moonflower, beginning to give off its dense nocturnal scent, arrived disquietingly, like desire radiating from a young body, close by in the summer twilight.

JOSÉ MARÍA IZQUIERDO

Small, dark, dressed in black, with questioning melancholy eyes, his face elongated by dark, pointed sideburns. Always in the library at the Atheneum, writing the articles for the daily papers through which he flung his talent into the street, when he wasn't slipping across the morning court-yard of the university or on the way back from the river and his evening walk.

He seemed to have no home, those four walls to enclose himself in solitude with his memories and hopes. Late at night you'd find him sometimes in a side street, coming from the rooming house where he lodged, looking defeated, sad and darker than ever. Because in that house he was to die, after a few days when he wasn't seen any-where, a definitive death; he, who as if in an interim life, was perhaps awaiting better times.

His love for poetry, for music—what good would it do those people who surrounded him? With less talent and cul-ture, with inferior spiritual qualities, others had obscured him from view of the Spanish public. Why did he persist like a caged bird in his provincial corner, standard bearer of a local cohort for the sake of a few friends who couldn't understand him?

Now, with those days and that land far away, I think it was all because of misplaced love: love for a city with a glorious past, whose spirit perhaps he wanted to revive, giving it everything he had, sacrificing his name and his work.

Yes, Bécquer and Machado left it behind. José María Izquierdo never abandoned it. In the end, who knows? During his hours of silent retreat, listening to music or in his evenings by the river, absenting himself from the noise of the others under his native sky, perhaps he enjoyed a greater and purer glory than anyone.

MUSIC AND THE NIGHT

Sometimes, around dawn, I'd be awakened by the plaintive strumming of a guitar. It was some young guys in the narrow street, still on the prowl with the night's energy, or maybe the mild weather or just the noisy restlessness of their youth.

Have you ever seen a child trying to seize a ray of sunlight? It was that pointless and mad, the urge that came over me lying in bed, in the solitude and calm before dawn, when I heard that music. It was life itself I longed to seize and press close to my heart: ambition, dreams, the love of my youth.

And what made my desire even more intense was the contrast between the fever surging in my veins and the nocturnal calm and quietness: as if life had nothing more to offer than this glimpse of its form, the tempting flight of happiness and pleasure.

The guitar's voice faded going up the street, quieting as it turned the corner. Like a wave swelling out of the sea to break in iridescent drops, my fervent longing burst into sobs; yet they weren't tears of sadness but of fullness and adoration. No subsequent disappointment has ever been able to dampen that passion. Only death's lips with their kiss have the power to quench it, and who knows if it isn't that kiss alone where human desire will one day find life's only possible fulfillment.

WALLED CONVENT

The big gate. The arches. (For an Andalusian, happiness always waits on the other side of an arch.) The white walls of the convent. The little windows blinded behind thick bars.

The rusty hinges creaked, and a damp mist assailed the visitor advancing step by step across the ground with its patches of grass dotted yellow here and there with weedy flowers. In the pond the green water reflected the sky and the leafy branches of an acacia. Above the eaves the swifts crisscrossing quickly, their chirping muffled in the cracks of the bell tower.

Along the gallery, after you called discreetly outside the convent window, a female voice could be heard, flat like the sound of an old cowbell: "Deo gratias," it said. "Thanks be to God," we answered. And the candied egg yolks, the citron or sweet potato sugar cookies, the work of anonymous bees in habits and wimples, would appear in a little white box from the mysterious shadows of the convent, as a gift to the profane palate.

In the hazy crepuscular light, in the silence of that hidden corner, the sublime food was beyond anything earthly, and taking a bite felt like tasting the lips of an angel.

NIGHTTIME SORCERY

Outside the city, the summer night eddied in quiet pools. Along the road to the inn, above which the acacias crossed their limbs, the jingling of bells betrayed the approaching carriage, and then it passed by slowly, its top open, and the intertwined legs of that couple just barely visible, darkness and solitude, with the driver's complicity, favoring their caresses.

The two were anonymous in the rocking carriage, lifted by desire into a class where names don't matter, because the act excludes them, transforming their private darkness into a whole symbolic image of life. Intertwined, not in love — who cares about love, that unruly and useless pretext of desire — but in pure animal pleasure, they fulfilled the ritual ordained by the species, of which the two were a plaything both freed and subjugated at the same time.

And so they were lost in the distance, the bells' jingling fading away after the sound of the wheels had gone, and night, thick, warm and mysterious, closed once more over the furrow they had opened. But in the leafy darkness, above which the stars hung sparkling, their image and their memory stayed with you to be treasured. And aren't that image and that memory what make for night's timeless enchantment, where the echoes, the voices (how sweet the voices of lovers sound at night), the footsteps of long-gone lovers seem to resound?

DESTINY

In the old building at the university there was, beyond the big patio, another smaller one, behind whose arches, among oleanders and lemon trees, a fountain murmured. The mad bustle of the main patio, once you climbed a few stairs and traversed a gallery, was changed there into silence and stillness.

One May afternoon, the whole building quiet, because classes were over and exams were near, you were strolling along the galleries of that hidden patio. There was no sound but the water in the fountain, light and steady, accented at times by the fleeting trills of a flock of swallows crossing the sky, which was framed by the building's eaves.

Through your whole life how many things have you not been told by the sound of water. You could spend hours just listening to it, the same way you could spend them gazing into a fire. Such a beautiful brotherhood, water and flame! That afternoon, the jet that sprang up like a white heron to fall back as tears into the fountain pool, its perpetual gushing and plunging, triggered in your memory, by some vague set of associations, the end of your time at the university.

The passing of generations never seems more melancholy than when it's embodied materially, like in those old university buildings or the dormitories, through which new youth is moving every year, leaving an echo of their voices and the crazy surge of their blood. The ambience brims with memories of youth gone by, and the walls resound in the silence like the hollowed-out spiral of a sea shell.

Leaning against a column in the patio, you thought about your future, about the need to choose a career, you, to whom all careers were equally repugnant, when all you wanted to do was escape that city and its lethal atmosphere. Your needs and your desires were contradictory, your poverty tying you to both with no solution. But how could such a petty problem matter at all when you saw yourself dragged along by the unstoppable flow of time, rising with one generation of people only to fall again, lost with them in the shadows? Deprived of joy, of pleasure and freedom like all the others, you understood then that maybe society has masked with false material problems humanity's real problems, to keep us from noticing our melancholy fate and the desperation of our helplessness.

SHADOWS

He was fair and slender—with a child's face, I'd add, if I didn't remember that ill-tempered look in his blue eyes of someone who's tasted life and found it bitter. On his shirt cuff, red as a fresh wound, he wore a braid, made in Morocco, where he'd come from.

He was atop a wagon, unloading bales of gold straw for the horses, who were inside, impatient, sheltered like plutonic monsters in huge dark vaults, wounding the stones with their hooves and rattling the chains that tied them to their stalls.

His distant, self-absorbed attitude, in the humble nature of what he was doing, recalled the young hero of some Oriental tale who, exiled from the family palace where all those slaves stood by to serve his slightest desires, knows how to turn himself to their work without giving up his own imperious grace.

*

He passed by one late afternoon, his round head covered with short black curls, a mocking grin sketched on his fresh mouth. His lithe, strong body, with its rhythmic bearing, brought to mind the Hermes of Praxiteles: a Hermes who carried in the crook of his arm, balanced against his waist, instead of the infant Dionysus, a huge watermelon, white stripes streaking its dark green rind.

*

Those creatures whose beauty we admired one time, where are they now? Fallen, tarnished, defeated, if not dead. But the eternal miracle of youth continues, and at the sight of some new young body, sometimes a certain resemblance awakens an echo, a trace of the other we loved before. Only when we remember that between one and the other there's a distance of twenty years, that this one hadn't even been born when the first still carried the bright inextinguishable flame the generations pass from hand to hand, an impotent pain assaults us, comprehending, behind the persistence of beauty, the mutability of bodies. Ah, time, cruel time, which tempts us with today's fresh rose only by destroying the tender rose of yesterday!

THE SHOPS

Those little shops were on the Plaza del Pan, behind the
Church of the Savior, where the Galicians parked, seated on
the ground or leaning against the wall, their empty sacks on
their shoulders and a handful of cords in their fist, waiting
for a trunk or a piece of furniture to move. The shops were
tucked into the church's wall, some defended by a little
glass door, others with their shutters wide open on the
plaza, and closed only at night. Inside, behind the counter,
silent and solitary, a neat little old man, dressed in black,
stood weighing something in a tiny scale with intense con-
centration, or a woman in lunar white, her hair pulled into a
knot with a comb stuck in it, was slowly fanning herself.
What were those merchants selling? In the dark rear of the
shop you might just catch a glimpse of something gleaming
in a display case, a vase with complex patterns of gems and
filigree and the purplish teardrops of some long coral ear-
rings. In others the merchandise was lace: delicate strips of
spun spray, hanging the length of the wall on a background
of yellow or sky-blue paper.

On the plaza, the Galicians (a designation by trade
not geography, as some of them were from Santander or
León) were hunched over, soft and tired-looking, more
from the weight of years than the thankless loads their work
condemned them to. They were the ones who, during Holy
Week, at the height of the brotherhoods, could be seen with
their clenched faces peering out from behind the velvet
platforms, shouldering the gold mass of statues and cande-
labras and bouquets, lined up like slaves along the benches
of a galley. Beside their painful superhuman labor with no
shelter but the pavement where they were parked, the aris-

tocratic merchants seemed to belong to another world. But they also subtly belonged together, like vestiges of a vanished day and age. In the little shops the silks and precious gems no longer sparkled, and the shoppers scarcely stopped there anymore. But in their seclusion, in their stillness, shopkeeper and porter alike were descended from the merchants and artisans of the East, and as the day wound down outside their door, the customer, in order to take home the amphora or the tapestry they'd just bought, had to seek out amid the bustle of the square the person big and strong enough to haul the merchandise.

In those little shops on the Plaza del Pan every one of the objects on display was still something unique, and therefore precious, crafted with care, sometimes right there in the back room, in accordance with a tradition passed from generation to generation, from master to apprentice, and it expressed or strove to express in an ingenuous way something fine and distinctive. Their drowsy atmosphere still seemed at times to flare up with the pure fire of the metals, and an aroma of sandalwood or faint perfume to float there vaguely like a trace of something someone had left behind.

MUSIC

Late afternoons in winter, two or three times a month, members of the concert society, like romantic conspirators, would move toward the theater through the streets where the lights were just coming on, in the opposite direction from people blurrily returning home from work. The lights came up on the red and gold décor of the rundown concert hall bedecked with that strange flower or fruit called the human face, most of them indifferent, some curious, a few expectant.

That's where I first heard Bach and Mozart; that's where music revealed to my senses its *pur délice sans chemin* (a line from Mallarmé, whose poems I was reading then), discovering what was for humans a form of flight, which our heavy nature denies us. Being young, a bit shy and overly impassioned, what I asked of music was wings to escape from those strange people surrounding me, from the strange customs they imposed on me, and who knows, maybe even from myself.

But one has to approach music more purely, and desire of it only what it can give us: contemplative bliss. In a corner of the hall, eyes fixed on one luminous point, I sat absorbed listening to it, like someone gazing out to sea. Its harmonious ebb and flow, its shimmering multiplicity, was like a wave that swept the soul right out of you. And like a wave that might lift us from life into death, it was sweet to be lost inside it, rocked toward the farthest edge of oblivion.

THE SEA

As night fell, in the summer, the train was rolling south toward the Atlantic coast. It was dark in the compartment, and past the window sped a landscape of prickly pear and olive trees, under a blue-green sky where only a red sliver of moon burned on the horizon like a piece of metal.

The train went up a grade, then twisted around a sharp curve. Suddenly the sea appeared below, in the ravine, and on the sea a narrow strip of land at whose tip stood a city: a tiny white profusion of little towers and terraces, surrounded by water. Was it the legendary sunken city sprouting from the sea's breast at that silent hour? Was it the cup of a water lily opening to the kiss of the twilight air? The sea was a deep dark blue, and everything seemed still, as if time were trying to hold itself in a spell that would never end.

Night had fallen when the train pulled into the coastal town, and you could barely make out its crooked walls, its rows of little white shacks and pairs of lovers close together whispering in the doorways, the greenish light of the gas lamps glowing from the patios. Steep narrow side streets led down to little silent squares, and from somewhere just out of sight, nearby, with a thick and bitter smell, came a long, strange, rhythmic sound, like that of huge wings beating, unable to fly.

At the foot of the sea wall your footsteps finally sank in the sand, and through the black air, like hazy ghosts, rose the sails of the fishing boats. And there he was: in the dark, a moan of pain or pleasure—a sleepless voice calling who knows what or to whom in night's nameless immensity.

LEARNING TO FORGET

April and May evenings, in the early hours, walking along the fence of the Retiro, you headed up that silent street where rows of acacias lined the length of both sidewalks. With the frequent rains there that time of year, their wet flowers, fallen, walked-on, gave off a fragrance that pervaded the air, your imagination connecting it with the way whiteness contrasts against the dark: the petals on the ground, the streetlights through the trees, the stars in space.

You climbed the front steps of your house and entered the living room (soft light, familiar voices, piano whose keyboard someone's hand stroked languidly), desiring both the presence and the absence of a certain person, the whole reason for your existence at the time. There was no way of masking your amorous obsessions; yet the mundane triviality, since that's all you had to work with, served as a kind of discipline, and so relieved for a little while the torment of the inflamed passion stabbing hour after hour, day after day, deep inside your mind.

And you smiled, you talked—about what? with whom?—like anyone else, although before long you had to shut yourself in a room, lying all alone on a bed, going over again in your memory the episodes of that sordid and sad affair, without the calm to sleep through the night, without the strength to face the day. It existed and waited, not even outside but inside you, where you didn't dare look, like some chronic physical illness that rest can relieve without its ever curing us completely.

Through the open balcony, beyond which at a distance spread the park's thick foliage, the smell of the rain-drenched acacias drifted in again, even more specific and insistent, and the stars seemed clearer and closer than before, seen from below in the street. Which was the dream? The inner suffering or the outer pleasure, of skin, the sense of smell, feeling the cold, still-clean caress of the predawn air bearing the scent of flowers and the dampness of rain, in the human springtime?

SUMMER

What amazing lightness filled your body waking on summer mornings, the generous heat still tempered in those early hours, when you'd go outdoors drunk on air, over the ground where golden shadows danced, and walking seemed on the verge of becoming flight. Winged almost, like a god, you met the day.

A full day of doing nothing awaited you: the ocean in the first hours, a lucid blue still cold after dawn; the poplar grove at noon, its friendly shade shot through with glittering light; the back streets as the afternoon wore on, strolling down to the port until you found a little café to sit in. Such marvelous idleness, thanks to which you were able to live your time, the moment completely present, whole and without regrets.

A few jasmine or spikenard flowers, placed on your pillow to freshen the night, brought back the memory of the kids who sold them, the bouquets strung on prickly pear leaves, the vendors no less delicate, nor their brown skin less smooth, than the petals of the flower watching over your sleep.

And you fell into darkness with a pleasure equal to the one you felt when giving yourself to the light, the whole perfect day settling over you gently as a folded wing.

THE LOVER

The August night blurred the dark sea and the sky into a single vastness, from which the grayish line of the beach was set apart, like the beginning of an uncreated world. Along there, naked under my white clothes, I was walking alone, though my friends, swimming out in the ocean, were calling me to join them. And among all those voices, I could pick out one that sounded fresh and pure.

The sea still held the day's heat in its breast, exhaling it in a warm and bitter breath that mingled with the night air. I walked a long while down the dark beach, filled with happiness, with drunkenness, with life. But I'll never say why. It's madness to try to express the inexpressible. Can words explain flame and its heavenly heat to someone who's never seen or felt it?

Finally I dived into the water, which, barely disturbed by the ripple, with a calm motion drew me out to sea. I could see in the distance the grayish line of the beach, and the white spot of my clothes where I'd dropped them. When my friends came out of the water, calling my name in the night, looking for me near the pile of clothes, inert like an empty body, I watched them unseen from the darkness, as if from another world and another life we might be able to watch, already without us, the place and the bodies we loved.

CITY ON THE PLATEAU

Between the snowy sky and the snowy plain, slicing through like a ship's prow, stood the city, its mass animating with a yellow halo the landscape's inhuman lack of color. Everything appeared in black, gray and white, even the shiver of water imprisoned in ice at the base of the turreted corner. Then the markets, the streets, the squares one after another, exalted by a self-contained radiance, which would sharpen at the cresting of some wall or the gable of a rooftop, while you wondered in vain where the solar source of that light originated.

It was shadowless, that light, not emanating from a distant star but springing just as brightly from here below, from earthly human stone, with those subtle shades, those unexpected shimmerings of a sea shell, a flower or a feather, where light appears to have left its trace delicately imprinted in the material. And you thought: gray goes with the Gothic, red with the Baroque, but with the Romanesque goes yellow; the blond, honeyed, amber, golden stone that the Romanesque, careless or unconscious of its own beauty, like a boy's rough body, is forever informed by.

That's how you saw the city and that's the way you loved it. Seat of activity and laziness, alone with history, encastled in its buttresses, under whose jutting eaves eternal time and deep reality built their nests, where tirelessly one day after another returns. Its stone, which even though set in civilized forms has no need to renounce its roots in untouched nature, is strong; but the light is stronger, and there light is the crown and foundation of stone.

SAINT

You were in Alba, and you didn't remember her being there until, in the solitary nave of the convent, there in the darkest corner, a little window opened like a trap door, revealing the underground cell where, lit by candles in her resting place, shrouded in her Carmelite habit among rag flowers, there was—a doll or a nun? Nothing and no one visible set the stage of this fantastic vision.

Suddenly, persuasively, and fundamentally impossible like a magic trick, everything was real or could be. Even the cured strips, remotely akin to limbs or intestines that once existed, set in silver in their respective cases, seemed to impose their reality, or at least confirm it, as much as they provoked your nausea. But the Spanish emphasis thus disfigured, in morbid caricature, the actual miracle.

Only those violets, resting beneath a ray of sunlight on the mantel of the village inn, concealed among their petals the myth of some elusive existence. Their color, their freshness, their scent, were true signs, not mummified this time, of the peerless creature, free of her commercial restoration, exposed to the rain, the dust, the wind of the roads, which cared less what she had done than what she was.

A life that neither needs nor asks for a stage, much less one of mortal corruption, but only to be left to infect her own kind with her deathless desire, subtle and strong, hidden like a flower pressed inside the solitude of a book, from which her presence creates the distant shore, the root beside the surface of the original water flowing in streams and torrents to nourish a naturally heavenly thought. And as in another time, when she was alive, her pen poised, her mind was thinking, listening to that great rush of water, that sound of rising rivers, water cascading, with lots of birds and whistling, and not in her ears but high inside her head, where it's said something loftier than the soul resides.

THE STORM

In the witches' pine grove, steep terrain, enormous trees, menacing sky, where the hundred-year-old branches instead of offering shelter seemed to form a hostile alliance with the storm, the first thunderclap broke far away, setting off others, like an avalanche of stones sent rolling down slopes and ravines, tumbling in a rush down a mountainside. Who was frightened first, alarming your companion, you or your horse?

From centuries past some ancestral fear flooded your consciousness faced with what wasn't impossible to consider, in its noise and violence, something like the wrath of creation and its hidden god, coupling the elemental instinct of being with the elemental forces of the earth. Everything came together to confirm the legend of so many Saturday gatherings in that grove, whether incidental, like the thunder and lightning, or consubstantial, like the scowling ruggedness of the spot.

The lashing rain turned the covering of even the thickest canopy useless as its silvery torrent poured through the branches, then, hitting the ground, dividing into rivulets spilling downhill. It seemed best to try to escape with the current rather than wait for it to blow over, as if the swiftness of your getaway on horseback could leave behind the thunder and drenching rain. But there were those who let you go on ahead of them, waiting on the ridge for a break in the clouds, under that black sky, which was giving off a yellowish steam.

Everything grew quiet as the sun began to set, though in a wild pause of unspeakable enchantment you could still hear the sound of the water slipping off the leaves and slapping the ground, which was soft and muddy under your horse's hooves. And with the light came the call of a cuckoo, and then another answering, or was it an echo, their winged dialogue crisscrossing the late afternoon, until the gleaming light and the whistling seemed to fuse in the air, as earlier the lightning and thunder were united.

Then you dismounted again, this time not to wait out the storm but to bid it goodbye and look around to see reborn a calm from which man seemed alien, but that the witches no doubt, generous for a moment to the traveler through their woods, allowed you to live through and get to know before returning to town and its people, still shaken, wet and happy.

WAR AND PEACE

Surely the station should have been bustling, crowded with life, all the more so for being the last stop before the border; but when you arrived there that February night it was dark and deserted. Seeing light behind a window down toward the corner of the empty platform, you were drawn that way.

It was the café. And it was so peaceful in there. So quiet. A woman with a child in her arms was sitting beside the fire. You could hear the muffled, calming rustle of the flames inside the stove.

You ordered toast and a glass of milk, with the diffidence of one who feels he's demanding the moon. And seeing your order taken without disdain, you were encouraged to ask for a few cigarettes as well.

Seated in the midst of such recovered peace and quiet, to exist felt like a miracle to you. Yes, it turned out everything was possible again. A chill shook your body, as when we come to our senses after a danger we hadn't noticed.

It was life anew; life, with the certainty it would always be this peaceful and profound, with the possibility of its going on as always, routinely, and promising no surprises.

*

Back there your bloody country lay in ruins. The last station, the station on the other side of the border, which separated you from it, was just a skeleton of twisted metal, its walls and windows gone—an unburied skeleton abandoned by the day's last light.

What can one man do against so much madness? And without looking back or pretending to know the future, you went out into the alien world from your own land, now so mysteriously strange.

PANTHER

That slender velvety blackness, which seems to weigh nothing more than what's needed to set itself against the air in autonomous resistance, paces endlessly behind the bars, beyond which those seduced by such ruthless beauty have stopped still to regard it. Its material strength has been refined to a commanding grace, and its will constructs, as in a dancer, a perfect physical equilibrium, each muscle lightly and precisely organized according to the musical and mathematical rule informing its every movement.

No, neither basalt nor granite could depict it, only a slice of night itself. Airy and light just like the night, vast and dark the same as the space from which some cataclysm flung it to earth, that blackness is illumined by the pale green light of its eyes, flashing at times with desire to rip and crush, the sole idea burning in the mental mass of its boredom. What poet or demon ever hated so much or so well the encircling vulgarity of man?

And when that lightning passes, focusing then on some other reality beyond what can be seen, its glance becomes indifferent to the offensive spectacle outside. Caught behind bars, its destructive power takes refuge beyond appearances, and that appearance which its eyes don't see, or don't wish to see, so close but inaccessible to the paw, the animal's thought now bloodlessly destroys, more perfectly and completely.

LOVE

They were at the edge of a little hill. They were three young poplars, with slender trunks, a light gray, standing against a background of pale sky, their white and green leaves fluttering on the slim branches. And the landscape's air and light in their calm beauty heightened the loveliness of those three trees.

I went to see them often. I sat before them, my face to the midday sun, and while gazing at them, little by little I felt a kind of beatitude filling me. Everything surrounding them was tinted, as if that landscape were a thought, with a serene classical grace: the hill where they stood, the plain from where you could see them, the grass, the air, the light.

Some clock, in the nearby city, tolled the hour. Everything was so lovely, in that silence and solitude, that tears of tenderness and admiration rose up in me. And this surge of feeling, anchored in turn in the clear outline of the three poplars, drew me toward them. And since no one else was around, I trustingly approached their trunks and hugged them, just to press to my own chest a little of their fresh green youth.

CALEDONIA CITY

Everything in this country, it and the land it sits on, seems unfinished, as if God had left it half done, distrusting his own handiwork. And as with the country, so the city. This city has been your prison for several years, useless in your life except for work, parching and consuming what youth you had left, with no entertainment or exterior stimulation, equally arid in people and things. Like the city, with its soot-stained red facades, repeated in diminishing perspective, one Chinese box enclosing another, and then another, and another, so its inhabitants: utterly repellent monotony and vulgarity. How to fill the hours of this bottomless existence?

A two-faced divinity, utilitarianism and Puritanism, is what gives such people culture, and sin for them means no material gain. Imagination is as alien to them as water to the desert, incapable of all free and generous superfluousness, the reason and very purpose of existence. And there in the depths of your being, amid your cruelest instincts, you find you wouldn't know how to condemn a dream: the destruction of this pile of bureaucratic cubicles. Maybe that would be a benevolent act, a just retribution for nature and life, so unknown, insulted and degraded here.

RIVER

Watching spring return to this island, a swan's nest in the middle of the ocean, remembering the clouds and rains of months past, you understand how the greenness of the leaves can be so light, so clear, so nearly liquid now. It wasn't light but water that made them bud, bringing with them, instead of a trace of light, as in sunny climates, a trace of hidden waters. And so, fragile, translucent, they cover the branches of those elms in the fluvial afternoon, and stirred by the wind, though the sea is far off, they breathe a breath of the sea.

But the water is here, at the base of the trees, all a gentle green matching that of the leaves, in the river, where in the distance a fleet of island swans is sailing; and lighter still, sliding along more easily than the birds, some slender rowboats sharp as arrows, propelled by young rowers — or archers? — stripped to the waist, creating with a nimble rhythm their own aquatic wakes.

Seeing them streaming away like that provokes a double desire, because joined with your admiration for their youth is a nostalgia for your own, now gone, achingly drawn away from you into them, who now possess it. Love slips off into the green current, lashed by the desire to possess again, with and by way of the desired creature, the time of that smiling and coveted youth, which the springtime rowers, as if eternally, carry away with them.

THE BLACKBIRD

A gray March day goes down among the naked elms, though over the grass, where the asphodel and the hyacinth are sprouting, the saffron's corollas are open, burning with a color just like that of a cheek stung by this chilly air. Close by, from some leafless treetop or some eave, tossing its sorrows over its shoulder, with heartfelt irony a blackbird sings.

Its song now has the same chirpy unshadowed lightness it had this morning, and retiring after a day in flight it holds in its throat the same joyous voice as when it woke. For it the light of sunset is identical with dawn, the repose of its warm feathers curled in the nest identical with its crazy crisscross darting through the sky collecting material for so many whistled strophes.

Out of the sky it brings to earth some heavenly seed, a bit of light moistened by dew, with which it seems to nourish its existence, not of a bird but a flower, and that's the source of those clear liquid notes flying out of its throat. Just as the violet fills the March air with its scent, the blackbird fills the March earth with its voice. And much like the dialectical opposition of spring and winter expressed in the weather of those days, the bird's song conveys the tension of passion and mockery.

As if death had ceased to exist—what could death matter to a blackbird?—as if death with its sharp heavy arrowhead couldn't touch it, the bird sings cheerfully, free of all human reason. And its infectious joy catches in the spirit of whoever's listening, creating from this spirit and that song, as from light and water, a single ethereal fullness.

THE HEATH

Look, this is the heath. Back in your childhood your imagination envisioned it, never doubting—how could a child doubt his imagination?—that the heath could only be as you created it, with that interior gaze that fills solitude, and so seen definitively. The word surprised you in the pages of a book, and you fell in love with it, associating it with gusts of wind and rain out of some unknown Northern sky. The vision was real and true, all dense, profuse, mysterious countryside; but in that landscape, as in a dream, there was no color whatever.

Time was to add color, when under foreign skies, weary and bored, you saw one day that moorland covered with sullen green bushes, which the summer set flowering with purple blossoms (there was no white heather there), so the fall could then turn them rosy, until withering little by little, they'd blend into that basic green their sad and monotonous dullness. That's when you understood the vividness of imagination's reality, and how much it can add to what you've read, however slight the plot on which it plays and builds.

Time, while applying color, removed enchantment, and a lot of time had now passed, when your intimate reality finally met the other one. So many things like the heath could speak to you before, and now that you faced them they were mute and expressionless—or was it you?—because heather is a plant of desolate and solitary places. Then, after a long look at the countryside and the sky, attuned in their grim appearance, with a vague satisfaction, more for the proof you were finally observing than for the problematic enchantment of the heath, you crossed disillusioned past its frontier flowers from summer into fall.

And you told yourself that when visible reality seems more beautiful than the one you imagined it's because a lover's eyes are seeing it, and yours weren't now in love, at least not at that moment. Imaginary creation trumped reality, and while that might mean nothing with respect to the beauty of the actual heath, there was more love in the child's vision than in the grown man's reasoned contemplation, and the pleasure of the former, in its fullness and beauty, had exhausted the future prospects of the latter, however real they were or seemed to be.

LIBRARY

So many books. Rows of books, galleries of books, panoramas of books in this vast graveyard of thought, where everything's now equal, and the fact that thought dies doesn't matter. Because books also die, though nobody seems to notice the smell (perhaps there's a lot of French literature here, with its trends reeking of death) exhaled by so many volumes slowly rotting on their shelves. Was this what they, their authors, had in mind?

Here's where immortality ends up later, where bitter hours of what was living settle, and the solitude of then is the same as now: nothing and no one. But a book should be a living thing, and its reading a marvelous revelation after which the reader is not the same, or is more than what he was before. If a book isn't this, its understanding is pointless, since knowledge takes up space, enough to displace intelligence, the way this library took the place of the land it stands on.

Don't let reading be for you, as it is for so many people who frequent libraries, an exercise in dying. Shake that barbarous intellectual dust from your hands, and leave this library, where your own thought could one day end up stored and mummified. You still have time and it's a perfect afternoon for going down to the river, where young bodies are swimming in the water more instructively than most books, including yours. Oh, to redeem on earth, whole and self-sufficient as a tree, all those excessive hours spent in reading.

THE OLD WOMEN

Look at them. It won't take long to convince yourself that they're not just ghostly illusions. They appear suddenly, and you don't notice them until you're right up close, without their looking at anyone, submerged in their own existence as if it depended on total concentration, on an act of will absorbed in its own continuity. There they are, on a park bench, or in front of a doorway or on a street corner, dramatic, fragile, ludicrous, stuck by their stiff joints in rigid positions, alone with a solitude that neither wants nor is able to tolerate the deceptions of company.

It's not just their bodies, if you can call that a body, the desiccated remains of what once was human, which in them only repels. It's also the unreal clothes they're wearing, which make them look like objects in some macabre museum: featherless hats with crows and strips of tape; fringed shawls of balding fur; long flared skirts from which a hook-shaped shoe sticks out, bent like a boat run aground. But everything matches, down to the last detail, frayed gloves, bags with raised beadwork, the dress that was in fashion more than a century ago.

Around them floats an air of fetid perfume, like that of a chest of drawers in storage for many years, giving off a scent of something decomposed, evoking time past, which returns not as memory, but a presence, both useless and irrevocable. No one knows them, speaks to them or accompanies them, and seen like this, in the morning, in the late afternoon, because they seem to avoid full daylight, they are the image of absolute exile, sent far from home not in space but in time.

You could almost believe they'd escaped from the other world, still mischievous, horribly roguish in their

gloomy truancy. But when you walk across one of those lit-
tle graveyards that often surrounds a church here, in which
beings from bygone centuries still retain a little piece of
earth, a few blades of grass and the luxury of a name, aston-
ished at the abundant sum of years lived by each of them,
you understand that these spectral old women might well
be creatures that death forgot. If traditional, empirical soci-
ety, to which they belong, hasn't already found for them a
definitive cure for incurable death.

WAYS OF LIVING

All your life, if it ever occurred to you to covet the good luck of someone else, it wasn't the power (by divine right or democratic vote, if not conquered by bloodshed) of those who govern men: it was freedom, that independence in the world enjoyed by certain fortunate ones. Their lives, imagined in the reading of so many stories and in relief against a magical childhood backdrop (Andersen or *The Thousand and One Nights*), at once wandering and centered, with something of the dignity pleasure can have and of the grace possessed by intelligence, passed before your interior gaze like an endless series of gratified desires in a noble atmosphere.

Your fortunate ones escaped from winter to travel to sunny climes: a sea voyage along southern coasts, among ruins on a fabulous shoreline dotted with olive trees, palms and oleanders, where traces of the gods were still in evidence. Then they returned home, to the ancient groves, the paths at the end of which could be glimpsed, reflected in a pool, the sharp outline of a Palladian villa, adapted with time's passage to the air there, humid and overcast. Beautiful books and bodies, music and friendship, creative work and leisure always surrounded them.

*

Then one time you had the occasion to see up close one of those people whose luck you thought you envied: Lord B., a kind of Don Sebastián de Morra, bald and pudgy, dressed indifferently, author of little songs, little poems, little novels, whose repute among others depended entirely on his social position. Two rooms in someone else's house afforded him temporary shelter, with this or that piece of his own glassware, porcelain or artwork to enhance the provided furnishings; his family home closed up to avoid expense; his travels, canceled by the war; for friendship and company, the weekly visit, paid for in kind immediately and eventually by mention in his will, of a fop resembling a character out of Petronius.

Yes, that was what you had coveted without knowing what it was, that life of a parasitic plant; a false life (like that *ballet russe* whose epoch was the apogee of such people, the first international of the grandly vulgar), cowardly and mangy, protecting for some distant heirs an increasingly besieged estate, and which resembled at best a vegetative condition, with its society gossip, its feeble little works, in the shadow of a crumbling empire. But if his life and others like it hadn't found it by now, where was that independence of a life without bonds or limitations? Where were the free wanderers in the world? Everywhere you look man himself is the greatest obstacle to his own destiny.

SPRING

This year you haven't met the awakening springtime in those fields, when under a gray sky, one early morning, you hear the impatient whistling of the birds, missing along the still bare branches the dew-damp leafy thickness that should be sheltering them. Instead of meadows sown with corollas of saffron, you have the filthy asphalt of these streets; and it isn't the air of March with its premature warmth, but the lingering chill that assaults you on your walk, freezing your bones at every street corner.

Lost in this gloomy reverie, nostalgically you stroll down a path in the park, where skittering along the ground in front of you, like some ghostly earthbound wing, blows one of last fall's leaves. It's so dried out and brown, you'd think it died years ago; its fresh green life gone, inconceivable, like the youth of that old man, motionless, on the other side of the railing, shoulders hunched, hands in his pockets, waiting for who knows what.

Then as you get closer, you see that the old man has at his feet bunches of early flowers, asphodels, hyacinths, tulips, of incredibly vivid colors in this frigid atmosphere. It almost hurts to see them like that, exposed in this northern setting, as if they too in their beauty would feel defenseless against the climate's dark hostility.

But there's the springtime, insanely generous. It calls out to your senses, and through them to your heart, where it comes in warming your blood and flooding your mind with light; and they in turn, at this magical invocation, despite the cold, the squalor, the lack of sun, cannot contain the vernal exuberance these flowers, with their promise, have brought you and infused into your apathy, your fear and your despair.

SNOW

Awakening to a strangely dark morning light, seeing through the window the fallen snow that's still falling, the familiar landscape hidden under it, you're overtaken by a wave of nausea, along with the desire to go back to sleep, where at least you'll be free of this waking nightmare. Snow sickens you in and of itself, and moreover for being symbolic of something insidiously sickening. But that something, what is it exactly? Neither its desolate breath, which gives your blood the chills, nor its scaly, viscous body, like a reptile's, suffices to explain the utter revulsion it inspires in you.

Its mystique has to do with a fireside ritual, when father, mother and children, as in some decorative print, exchange smiles and gifts around a dead pine tree, just like an altar, while outside snow encircles and traps them; this same cruel, sterile, inescapable snow. Here's one and not the least of the typical inconsistencies common to mass thought: to find one of the myths of life precisely where life itself is missing, unless this is a way of expressing an unconscious desire for the annihilation of human insignificance at the peak of its religious festivity.

Snow was once water, that marvelous fluid substance that flows in so many lovely forms: fountains, rivers, oceans, clouds, rain; all graceful, moving, restless, like life; coming and going, rising and falling, with its musical sound, its magic sparkle, its supreme freedom. But ice, killing it, stops all that; and there it lies still, its plumage lightless, its throat soundless, its wings stripped of their air, what was the sweetest delight of existence, at least of your existence, you who so loved water, free-flowing, ever-changing water.

Is this, was this water? Like any creature the moment death has taken it, installing itself inside that now-strange form where we don't even recognize our friend, turning away suddenly in distrust that overcomes our old affection, that's how it is when water dies into snow. Is it that sudden emptiness of death, that mocking image of nothingness, that repels you, turning the world on its head and sending it back to the state before or after life, back to that mass of ice where man is merely his posthumous or unborn ghost?

LIGHT

When in those mornings your body was stretched out naked under the sky, a related power, animal and ethereal, the weight of being human refined and exalted by virtue of light, came into you with irresistible force. With its presence those elements that combine to make a body — water, air, earth, fire — were silenced, embraced in perfect harmony and proportion. Every form seemed to be gathered under a single name and every name seemed the origin of a form, with that pristine precision of creation: exterior and interior worlds corresponded and fit together as when lovers in their desire surrender to one another. And your body listened to the light.

If anything on earth can testify to the existence of some divine power, it is light; and some deep instinct brings a person to recognize in light that possible divinity, even though the essential calm that light diffuses brings with it an equivalent essential anguish, since death is defined from then on by the loss of light.

But if God is light, isn't the spirit's imperfect knowledge of it by way of the body bound to find perfection in God by way of death? As objects placed in fire are consumed, turned into flame themselves, so the body in death, in order to turn into light and become one with the light that is God, where there is no alternating light and darkness, but light complete and infallible. And even if that's not so, still your naked body in the sun on this earth once gathered and stored in its dark heart, desperate for solace, just enough bits of that illusory divinity to illuminate death, if death must be what finally defines us.

SOLITUDE

Solitude for you resides in everything, and everything for you resides in solitude. That happy island where so often you took refuge, entering more fully into life and its designs, bringing there, as one brings home from the market a bunch of flowers whose petals then unfold in shy exuberance, the turbulence that gradually would deposit its sediment of images and ideas.

There are those who in the midst of life gather it up in a rush, and they are the improvisers; but there are also those who need to distance themselves in order to see it better, and they are the contemplatives. The present is too rough and sudden, often enough full of ironic dissonance, and it makes sense to step back and find the perspective to understand its surprises and repetitions.

Between others and you, between love and you, between life and you, lies solitude. But that solitude, which separates you from everything, doesn't sadden you. Why would it sadden you? When you settle accounts with everything, with the earth, with tradition, with people, you owe none as much as you owe to solitude. A little or a lot, whatever you are, you owe it to her.

As a child, looking at the sky at night, whose stars resembled visible friends filling the dark with mysterious sympathy, the vastness of space didn't frighten you, on the contrary, it held you in a trusting fascination. There among the constellations shone yours, clear as water, brilliant as coal compressed into diamonds: the constellation of solitude, invisible to so many, evident and beneficent for some, among whom you've had the luck to count yourself.

THE PARK

On the grass, where empty benches line the avenue, tiny in the distance at the foot of the big trees, the morning light falls in shafts alternating with shadows. The trunks, seen in perspective, seem from a distance too fragile to sustain, though lightened by autumn, the mass of their branches, through which the light blue of the sky glimmers, accented here and there with pink or gray. A golden luster envelopes everything, harmonizing the various shades of green, less as a work of light than a work of weather layered in successive atmospheres. Nature left to itself gathers in its breast such calm and such beauty, generated and sustained one by the other, like the sound and sense in a perfect line of poetry.

In the afternoon, wind sweeps through the rows of trees something that in its winged swiftness could either be dry leaves or gold birds migrating. The air is mild, some of the trees still holding their green intact, pigeons fluttering as if driven by the energy of spring, and children come out with their tricycles, with their kites, with their sailboats. If the leaves didn't crunch underfoot, no one would say it was fall, not even that sickly dog who, envious and jealous, patrols the play of his young companions. The luminousness of a St. Martin's summer fills the afternoon with deceptive promises: the perfect weather presents a future delayed, with moments as full as the lengthening days of a whole spring that's just beginning. Over there among the farthest tree trunks, where a mist obscures the air's transparency, from the flame of that bonfire one would say autumn itself, in a sacrificial pyre, seeking transubstantiation, was ablaze.

*

This little square toward which the rising avenues converge appears in the hours before dawn to be the mouth of an extinct volcano, in whose center the red-eyed moon, strangely low and aflame, exposes the black water of the pond. How night's cold dampness chills the bones, stripping the flesh from the pedestrian and setting free his ghost. In such an otherworldly landscape, only the force of desire holds to their skeletons those embracing bodies of a couple on a bench, kept safe from another form of annihilation the malevolent powers of the red-and-black night inflict, sucking the blood from veins and replacing it with darkness.

THE BELLS

You'd like to know what it is about memory that makes it so seductive. Does the word memory itself signify all the timeless emotion of a conjuring that substitutes for the present in time a present of its own beyond time? Because that's what's so mysterious: that an emotion should be born from the shadowy recollection of something in memory that seemed to provoke no such emotion when it was actually happening, the way the light that reaches us from a star is not the light of that moment but the one that set out long ago from a distance. There are emotions, then, whose effect is not concurrent with their cause, and have to pass through the most vast and dense regions inside us, until one day we feel them. But why just then, and not before, or later? What's the balance between the power of an emotion and the resistance of our spirit?

You ask yourself this as you experience now, for no apparent reason, a delayed emotion flooding into the present, bringing with it, visible to your interior gaze alone, its own circumstances in space and time. Leaving aside the fact that perhaps the effect seems out of rational proportion to its cause, it's what returns to you now as the sound of those cathedral bells. Hearing them, back then, produced no emotion in you, at least none you were aware of at the time; but the magic with which they resound now in your spirit, free and apart from all explanation, seems to revive a euphoria of solemn and familiar festivity, meaningless to everyone but you.

No, it's not the idealization of something long ago, like an insect caught in amber, that so animates a moment from the past, because that sound and its surroundings weren't hidden as if deaf within you when you heard the sound of the bells, bound with some precious or beloved moment. The clarity of its impression, when you, entranced, the floodgates of the rest of your senses shut, contained the whole of life in one aural perception, useless then and useless now, works the belated spell of the evocation, making that afterimage more beautiful and meaningful than the reality. And from that you would conclude that the importance or value of an individual existence results not from its transcendent or happy circumstances but, however luckless or anonymous, the fidelity with which it has been lived.

THE ARRIVAL

Awake well before dawn, out of bed, showered and dressed, your bags packed, you took a seat in the empty salon. Everything, sitting rooms, corridors and the ship's deck, was deserted. Through the big windows just the murky blackness of ocean and sky, although the sea could always be made out by its sound, barely audible now, with the half habit acquired in the days of passage and the stormy impatience to reach a new land and city, long imagined. The light was slow in coming and it looked as if it would be a while until the coast could be seen.

Sitting for a good spell with your back to the row of windows, a feeling made you suddenly turn your head. And there it was: the outline of skyscrapers over the water, sketched in exceptionally subtle shades, a rose, a lilac, a violet like the colors inside a sea shell, all emerging from a gray background ranging from leaden to pearly. The tops of the buildings against the sky and the contiguous skyline were etched in yellow by an unseen sun, and on either side this axis of light was darkened by night and ocean at the highest and lowest reaches of the horizon.

You'd seen it so many times in movies. But now the coast and the city appearing before you were real; and yet, what an air of unreality they had. Was it you who were here? Was this before you the city you were expecting? It seemed so beautiful, more beautiful than anything you'd seen before in images and in your imagination; so much so that you feared it would vanish like a mirage, that the ship was still at sea, that you'd never arrive, condemned to wander perpetually, a soul without a body, between the windy abyss of the air and the raging abyss of the water.

But it was real: the countless annoyances with which people had learned and needed to surround the events of life (passports, permits, waiting in line, police interview, customs) were definitive proof. And more than seven hours later, the human animal's harassment completed, you could walk free of the customs shed on the dock into the light of midday: you finally set foot in the city you'd glimpsed, fabulous as a Leviathan, rising from the sea at dawn.

It seemed so mundane now, with the same dull streets and miserable houses as in that loathsome Scotland, left behind years ago. But these were just the outskirts; the real city was farther in, all stores with shiny and tempting window displays, like Christmas or saint's day toys, decked out with banners under a clear fall sky that brightened the colors, alive with the enviable joy of reckless youth. And you entered the rough and marvelous city, as if it were extending to you its hand brimming with promises.

HELEN

for María Dolores Arana

> I must confess that you surprised me yesterday
> when you stated that Spain, in its art, knows nothing of
> beauty.
> —On that question I have written pages where my
> opinion is made perfectly clear: Spain knows nothing of
> beauty because Helen never set foot there.
>
> (C. Mauriac, *Conversations with André Gide*.)

A friend was puzzled by your preference, among the
Spanish poets, for Garcilaso over Saint John of the Cross.
Garcilaso is one of those very rare writers of ours whom we
can call an artist. Free of mundane and superhuman com-
mitments (he never spoke of the Empire or of God), he
seeks beauty, with everything this search implies, and in his
search he needs nothing more than human faculties and
earthly means, which he possessed in abundance.

He had the good luck to live when the Renaissance
was burning and scattering with the ancient light of Greece
so many murky medieval fogs, a light that also reached, for
a strange and happy moment, as far as Spain—a moment
that was to be, unfortunately for us, as fleeting as a light-
ning flash. Soon, on account of the indigenous milieu and
temperament, Spain falls again into the medieval past, from
which it will never find its way out.

Garcilaso benefits from that light and that moment and
his poetry is nourished by it. For both, humanity is of this
earth and in it they discover, come to know and revere, as a
singular deity, Beauty. Most Spanish poets, given the
absence of native enthusiasm for thought or reflection, had
no interest in seeing what the great Racine saw: that when

the poet acquires or regains faith, what the Christian wants to say as a Christian may not be of interest to the poet, as a poet.

*

On another occasion you wrote: "I can't help but deplore the fact that Greece never touched the Spanish heart or mind, the most remote in Europe from and most ignorant of the 'glory that was Greece.' One sees this clearly in our lives, our history, our literature." What Spain thus lost forever wasn't only the knowledge of beauty, important as that is (and when as an exception the Spaniard seeks beauty, what clumsy lack of experience he betrays), but also the knowledge of and respect for moderation, one of its most significant attributes.

No one among us would have been capable of that beautiful desire for knowledge that, in Faust, on contemplating the face of Helen, admirable symbol of Greece, her country, could ask: *Was this the face that launched a thousand ships / And burnt the topless towers of Ilium?* In that magical face some few could summarize their whole belief in and love for this world. It's true that human beauty, according to the platonic principle, is nothing but a reflection of the divine. But hard as you might try, you could never reconcile Judeo-Christian divinity with Greco-pagan beauty. And if you had to choose between the two, you'd happily and rightly side with the latter.

HOME

You've always had the desire for a home, your home, to envelope you in a friendly atmosphere for work and for doing nothing. But at first you didn't know (because you would learn it later, after living among strangers) that behind your desire, and blended with it, was another: that of a refuge with the friendship of your things. Everything else would wait outside, but inside would be you and what was yours.

One day, when you'd already begun to wander the world, dreaming of your home but without one, an unexpected event at last presented you with the chance to have one. And you began to set it up around you, simple, comfortable, full of light: table, books, lamp—an atmosphere filled with the scent of the season's flowers.

But it was too easy, and your life too unsettled, to last very long. One day, another day, it disappeared as unexpectedly as it had come. And you went on wandering across so many lands, some that you hadn't even wanted to know. How many plans for a home you've had since then, nearly realized another time only to be lost again later.

Just four walls, a space as cozy as a ship's cabin, but yours and full of what's yours, even as you know its shelter could be transitory; light and silent and solitary, without the presence and the bothersome noise of those strangers with whom it's so often been your fate to share your living arrangements; tall, with its windows open to the sky and the clouds above the crowns of some trees.

But that's a dream you've abandoned now as impossible, even though for others it's a reality you can't aspire to. Your existence is too poor and always changing—you tell yourself, as you write these lines standing up, because you don't even have a table; your books (the ones you've kept) piled in a corner, like your papers. In the end, you don't have much time left, and who knows if it isn't better to live like this, stripped of possessions, perpetually ready for departure.

RETURN TO DARKNESS

After the exhaustion of an all-night journey, well past midnight with little sleep and that fitful, between feverish and chilled, you entered the hotel's dark and deserted lobby. What emptiness there is in that hour just before dawn; what an uncreated or extinguished world it is that one sees then.

Behind you remained those sun-drenched days by the sea, a time that was good for nothing apart from careless pleasure, the companionship of a creature you loved like nothing and no one else. The cold you felt was more that of his absence than it was of the early hour of an autumn daybreak.

Abruptly stripped of light, of heat, of company, you seemed to be walking disembodied into who knows what unearthly sort of limbo. And with mounting anguish you looked back toward that happy corner, those bright days, now irretrievable.

What agony there was in that desolate dawn, among the sordid objects of ordinary existence, made by and for those who can't be and will never be part of you. Entering into so much strangeness, your life—it too—became another inert and empty object, like a shell from which the pearl has been extracted.

And why not say it? Your tears spilled bitterly then, since you were alone and no one but you bore witness to such weakness, on account of what was lost. Lost? You yourself were the widower of your love, the loser and the lost one, all at the same time.

Won't it be possible to retrieve in another life those happy moments that have been so brief in this existence full of annoyances, tedium, strangers? Won't it be possible to reunite forever with the creature you loved so much?

("And to see you always, / Here before my eyes, / Without the fear or shock of losing you"). And if it's not possible, what's the point of living, when the one thing that kept you alive is already past?

Like Orpheus you would defy the fires of hell to rescue and bring back with you again the image of your happiness, the form of your delight. But there are no kindly gods who will return to us what we've lost, only blind chance which goes on tracing crookedly, like a staggering drunk, the stupid course of our lives.

SILENT CALL

With smiling affection, the way one thinks of a child's amusing fancies, you remember those little white ice cream trucks (though you were never that fond of ice cream) that appeared every evening along the boulevards and avenues of the city, happily sounding, to attract customers, their little music-box tune, so childish, delightful and trivial.

Sometimes you'd hear them from a friend's house, from a ground-floor room with its big sunny window open on the oceanfront avenue, shaded by palms and eucalyptus facing the sea. The marvelously happy blue sky passed little by little through all the shades of the sunset's kaleidoscope, tinting the air with indescribable shimmerings.

Other times you'd hear them from the upstairs window of your bedroom. Down below, in the deep canyon of the avenue, you could hear them coming from quite a ways off, until finally you'd make out the little white wagon sounding its pleasant melody. The sky came down in shadows, igniting below your window the magical festival of the city's lights, tracing a map in which you could make out and identify only the shining parts like the beacon atop the monstrous Mormon temple. And you could still hear that little music-box tune in the distance, at intervals, slowly approaching.

The memory of certain pleasant days, of a happy experience in our existence, can crystallize around a trivial object which, converted indirectly into a symbol of that memory, acquires a magical value. And still—this is the paradox—as easily as you can call up and inwardly picture the image of those little ice cream trucks, you can't on the other hand remember or hum to yourself the tune they played, that jingling song, now inaccessible, even though it keeps on sounding in your memory ideally, mysteriously, silently.

HARMONY

for Jacobo Muñoz

The bat and the blackbird can take turns debating which one rules your spirit—sometimes northern, solitary, immersed in reading, self-absorbed; at others southern, easygoing, sunny, in search of the moment's pleasure. But in either of these spiritual metaphors, always deeply susceptible to resonating in harmony, when harmony comes.

It began in your adolescence, and it never happened or happens of its own accord, but required or requires a stimulus. Stimulus or complicity? For it to happen you had to be swept away on a wave of sound, listening to music; but though it never occurs without music, music doesn't always, and very rarely, makes it happen.

Look at him: as a child, sitting alone and still, absorbed in listening; as an adult, sitting alone and still, absorbed in listening. He seems to be having—how to describe it?—a "mystical" experience. I know, I know: it's the wrong word; but there it is, whatever it's worth, for better or worse.

It's first of all—a slowing down? No, it's not that. The normal course of consciousness, the sense of existence, seems to grow feverish, until it glimpses, as in a vision, what hasn't yet occurred, but what ought to occur. Life intensifies and, filled with its own energy, reaches a point beyond which it couldn't go without exploding.

As if a door had opened? No, because everything's already open: an archway into boundless space, where actual legend spreads its wings. And that's how one moves from the mundane world into the other strange and unusual one. One's personal situation is joined with a cosmic force, and one's emotion with the rapture of the elements.

The moment stays outside time, and in that timeless moment one glimpses the shadow of a timeless pleasure, a cryptic trace of all earthly pleasures, which might be within reach. Everything seems possible or impossible (at this intensity of existence what's the difference between winning and losing), and is ours or one would say it's about to be ours. Doesn't the outer music and the inner rhythm of the blood assure it?

A fullness that, recurrent through our life, always feels the same; not some atavistic memory, nor a foretaste of what's to come: but testimony to what it might mean to be fully alive in this world. The closest thing to it is the experience of entering another body in the act of love, in oneness with life by way of the lover's body.

You've said it before: you can neither perceive nor want nor understand a thing that doesn't come into you first by way of sex, and from there to your heart and then your head. And that's why your experience, your mystic harmony, begins as a sexual foreshadowing. But it isn't possible to seek it out or provoke it willingly; it's given only when and the way it wants to be.

Obliterating what's called otherness, you are, thanks to it, one with the world, you are the world. The word to describe this doesn't exist in our language: *Gemüt:* unity of feeling and consciousness; to be, to exist, purely, with no confusion. As someone once said who perhaps felt the same sort of thing, only toward the divine, as you toward the human, it's a long way from being to Being. And it's a long way from existing to Existing.

And the thing that leads from one to the other is this: harmony.

Variations on a Mexican Theme

THE THEME

for Manuel Rodríguez Lozano

Neither Larra nor Galdós, so different, yet of equally clear consciousness, ever concerned themselves with these other lands rooted in Spain. Faced with their break from the peninsula, Larra, a contemporary, and Galdós, a near contemporary, say nothing. Why? From the national vision each of them offers us, something is missing; something that had historically been part of our lives, and was torn away from it during the same century in which both lived and wrote.

How to understand this silence? As indifference? In Larra's case, given his willingness to probe in his own and his country's wounds, which are the same, any other reason to waste such a fine opportunity would seem strange. For Galdós, besides, perhaps there was some ill will, since his commentary concerned a past that was still too present not to provoke objections from his readers on this other side.

Some first, others soon after, within a very brief time, all these lands detached themselves from Spain. None of our writers mentions this break after that, neither to deplore nor even acknowledge it. If their accession left so few echoes in our classic literature, it makes sense that their separation would leave even fewer in our modern writing. And since no Spaniard would ever permit without agitated protest anything in our common national life that goes against his personal sense of things, if nobody said a word about this, nor took to the streets, it must have had nothing to do with them.

Spain, then, had not been, nor ever was for most of us, anything beyond the peninsula, and it seems that the Latin Americans,

---

Translator's note: Mariano José de Larra (1809-1837) and Benito Pérez Galdós (1843-1920), two of Spain's best-known nineteenth-century writers, were famous for their penetrating explorations of Spanish character and culture.

for their part, understood this before we did. Perhaps we Spaniards never took any interest in these other lands, which for centuries were part of our nation. (Cervantes, although he himself wanted to come, and could not, thought of those who did: "The Indies, refuge and sanctuary for Spain's desperate ones, church of the rebellious, safe passage for murderers, shelter for gamblers called right by the experts, all-purpose lure for free women, common deception of many and private cure for a few.")

But how to reconcile our evident national indifference, if not avoidance toward these lands, with the vigor embodied and the work accomplished by Spaniards there? With echoes of ourselves still resonating, still intact across time and distance, and so familiar? Perhaps it was all, like so much else in life, the work of just a few, faced with the hostility of others and the apathy of most?

*

In your childhood and youth, what did you know, if anything, of these lands, of their history, which is one with yours? You weren't even curious, admit it. Your own fault, no doubt; but nothing around you served to stir your curiosity. What you heard, when you heard anything, political rhetoric empty of thought and lacking all sincerity, was moreover enough to kill any curiosity. Nothing brought to life in your indifferent imagination the marvelous events, the work of a handful of men the likes of which haven't been seen before or since, nor the setting of their actions, although it was and is right here, so alive, so beautiful.

It was only life and its chance occurrences which much later aroused that curiosity in you, when you were face to face with American reality. And from curiosity came interest; and from interest, sympathy; and from sympathy, love. But a strange shyness made this belated love hard for you to express. A recognition of its uselessness? It is shyness, anyway, that now inhibits you, and leads you to skirt the theme.

VARIATIONS

THE LANGUAGE

"After crossing the border, on hearing your language, which you hadn't heard spoken in so many years, what did you feel?"

"I felt as if my life in it was continuing uninterrupted now in the outer world, since inwardly I had never stopped hearing it all those years."

*

The language our people spoke before we were born from them, the one that served us in getting to know the world and taking possession of things by way of their names, important as it is in anyone's life, it's even more so in the poet's. Because the poet's language is not just the material of his work but the very condition of his existence.

And if the first word your lips pronounced was Spanish, and Spanish will be the final word you speak, determined precisely and fatally by those two words, the first and last, are all those of your poetry. Since poetry, finally, is the word.

*

How not to feel pride on hearing our language spoken, a faithful echo of itself and at the same time the autonomous expression of other people on the other side of the world? They, knowing it or not, wanting it or not, with those same signs of their soul, which are words, are keeping alive our country's destiny, and will go on keeping it alive even after it should cease to exist.

Alongside that destiny, how narrow, how perishable seem those of other languages. And how grateful must the obscure artisan be to feel, alive in him, this language that's now his own, for whom four centuries ago, with pen and sword, its universal destiny was won. Because the poet cannot attain that destiny for his language without the hero's help, nor the hero attain it without the poet's.

MIRAVALLE

This wing of what was once a viceroy's palace has just one floor, and above it is all terraces. From its raised cliff, wherever you look, you see foliage below: first in the park, then along the avenues. In the background, a steel blue capped with snow, are mountains. And above them, sky, a deep and luminous sky.

All this being so new to you, still none of it seems foreign. There are probably more-beautiful places on earth, but none that so floods the soul of the beholder. Look, look closely: take in all this beauty whole, since its contemplation is a gift from destiny, when you were least expecting it.

These terraces, these galleries, are just a frame for the splendid landscape, barely containing it to make it accessible to someone's eyes, imperceptibly humanizing it. Spread out beneath the human gaze, it smiles back sympathetic, almost tenderly. Because its grandeur doesn't exclude the smile, nor the dramatic the delicate, as it's a landscape of conciliations, not extremes.

The tragic echoes of legend and of history these leaves and galleries hold are no match for the old desire for pleasure, for permanence, which once again this view inspires in you. Leaning against the railings, strolling under the arches, it seems impossible, were it given to you to stay here, that one day you'd feel satiated, and with that feeling man's ancient curse: the desire to move on.

DIGNITY AND REPOSE

In Anglo-Saxon countries people don't know how to relax, and their bodies don't adapt naturally to rest. Here on the other hand the postures of repose come naturally to bodies, so naturally that they can adapt even to the worst situations with grace.

Quick now. Before you forget, remember, among others, certain ones.

*

That kid in the doorway of a village convent, white clothes and straw hat, sitting on the bottom step, back to the wall, one knee up, his arm draped over it, hand hanging loosely with index finger extended, like Adam in the Creation fresco in the Sistine Chapel.

Or that other one, lying on a low wall surrounding a little garden in a plaza. His seat, or more precisely his sofa, was surely uncomfortable. And yet, how long had he been there, folded up like that with such spontaneous grace, his head resting on one arm and the other fallen along the length of his body?

*

The postures of women, in contrast, seem more austere, and it isn't their elegant casualness but their fierce dignity that catches your attention. Like that old Indian woman, all wrapped up in her faded blue rebozo, walking barefoot toward the church, as she could have marched, centuries since, to the sacrifice. Or the one squatting on the dusty ground, with the ritual expression of a priestess, cooking a little food by the roadside. No. The body in this land still maintains its natural dignity. And the consciousness of that bodily dignity manifests nowhere so well as in its carelessness.

COUNTRY MUSICIANS

Into the farmhouse courtyard comes the caretaker with his friends, and the guitar, which one of them carries half hidden. While they talk to us of the coming celebrations, of the impossible climb one of them will make to the rugged peak at whose base the town sits, night has been slowly falling. Through the arches you can barely see the garden now. Since the hour is ripe and there's still a little time, we ask for a song; that's what they came for, but they resist with timid courtesy. The one with the guitar at last begins to strum.

The guitar sounds good, the music flowing from it with a shy grace. And those strange falsetto voices leaping into the current of the melody. To your unaccustomed ear at first they seem out of tune; but then, beneath the apparent dissonance, you perceive a deeper harmony. There is, between the words and their falsetto singing, a subtle joke; fitting, when the lyrics are satirical; more fitting still when they're dramatic.

The smooth edge of their singing doesn't fool you. Rough as they are, these men, they're exalted by a cold passion you don't know how to thank them for. When, driving back at night along the dark highway, you see them appear in pairs before the headlights, white figures under the halos of their hats, with their serapes hanging to one side, the arm of one around the other's shoulder, weaving a little (you'd say) under the influence of pulque, you understand that that's not really why, but rather lyricism, which flowers in their flesh from their souls' depths. The pulque, at most, is just a pretext.

WHAT'S OURS

Barely across the border, in the first run-down, dusty town, where you saw those children begging for handouts, those young girls in black veils and dresses, the memories, painfully, were awakened in you. Memories of your country, also poor and also gravely ill. And you felt tempted to go back across, right then, to the other side you'd come from.

The first contact with those surroundings, which are your surroundings, was hard after all those years. All you could see were misery and desolation, against which you were trying to protect yourself, renouncing whatever possibilities, in spite of everything, they might present. Yet once you were past that initial reaction of atavistic resentment, you began to glimpse, to recover something very different.

That land was alive. And then you understood the whole value of that word and its full significance, because you had almost forgotten that you were alive. Maybe the price of being alive was this poverty and pain you could see all around; maybe life demands, in order to be alive, that base manure of misery and sadness, out of which, like a flower, it rises purified. Sophistry? Nothing remained there of the triviality and emptiness of life in the lands you were coming from.

Wealth at the cost of spirit? Spirit at the cost of poverty? It seems impossible to reconcile wealth and spirit. But it's not you, or perhaps anyone, who can choose. Think only, if what matters to you is spirit, where your sympathies lie. Without even making a rational choice, without the least hesitation, they fall instinctively on one side. Oh my people, mine in all their poverty and desolation, so alive, so belovedly alive.

WATERBORNE

Under the little boat's awning we glide along the canal, escorted by another one with musicians: guitar, violin, clarinet, maracas. On both sides tall slender trees, resembling poplars, which are said to grow only here, and narrower canals, some dry, flowing into this one where we're navigating. The sky, blue just before, is clouding over.

In this veiled light the water looks more turbid, the trees less healthy, the musicians older. An imminent decline threatens all this, so painfully beautiful. New land? You don't know what echoes of extinct wisdom, of relinquished life, are floating through the air. Those silent mysterious bodies, which as their boats pass by hold out a flower or some fruit, must know the secret. But they're not talking.

Rain pours down on the awning, and since the canal goes on forever, we disembark at a little bankside snack bar. There, where everything is disguised in contemporary banality, we almost forget the landscape's oppressive secret. But it lingers outside, under the sky, under the summer rain, under the gloomy branches, under the turbid waters, where the flower boats seem to offer occasional tribute to its sunken memory.

THE SIDEWALK

Early one night you were led by friends down the sidewalk of that street, lined on one side by noisy bars and little theaters, and on the other by fried-food stands. In between moved the jostling flow of bodies, many of them looking for a signal to connect, in search of more intimate contact. Down dark side streets, which appeared at intervals, you could also sense a baser brand of the same risks and temptations.

In the full light of the street you were surprised by one well-lit storefront, still open at that hour, which from a distance seemed to be neither a restaurant nor a tavern. Up closer, through the bright entryway, you suddenly saw stacks of coffins, as yet unlined with their metal sides, also awaiting their customers.

Like the sound of a final trumpet amid that crush of bodies, it was hard to tell if that curious juxtaposition signaled a more than human irony that seemed to go along with the surrounding liveliness. Later, when you saw the kinds of toys the children played with there, among them a figure of Death on horseback, a delicate work that revealed in its anonymous craftsmanship the instinct of a tradition, you began to understand.

The child in whose hands the representation of death was a thing to play with would grow up with a greater acceptance of it, stoical faced with its inevitability, a good son of what may be the most vital land of all, yet behind whose life death isn't hidden or disguised with shame, but recognized as part of life itself — or life, perhaps more accurately, seen as an inseparable part of it.

FLOWER VENDORS

Protestants, who cover the world with factories and whose lives are consumed inside them (productively, to all appearances), would laugh at those people who use their little bit of earth to grow some flowers. Standing or squatting by the side of the road, the women wrapped in their shawls, the men under big straw hats, a bunch of roses or carnations in each hand and others held in tin cans on the ground, waiting, always waiting.

Very few cars go by, possibly fewer than necessary, assuming they'd stop to buy flowers, for each person in the group to earn in a day's work a few miserable coins. But there they are, day after day, and when a customer does pull over, they approach the car without competing with each other, exquisite offerings in their hands—the shapes and colors and scents of the bouquets.

Under the wing of the sombrero, in one of those fresh faces just barely past being childlike, there's such intensity in that gaze. The lips are silent, but the eyes speak volumes, and how well they say it. Would Protestant industrialists be able to understand that poverty can be a proud and uncompromising profession? How do people exist who can't even say they prefer to be last, because for them there is no last or first?

The flowers just purchased, we'd like to leave them, along with the money, in those hands. The coins, as necessity's most minimal relief; the flowers, as insufficient tribute to the dignity of their lives, to the grace of their bodies, to the eloquence of their faces. Because beauty nourishes, and as with bread, a man can also perish from its absence.

THE OVERLOOK

In this corner of the convent, the ground an uneven surface of reddish bricks, a color just barely more ochre than that of the walls, the two arches where they come together opening on the landscape draw you to them, call to you from the corridor of the cloister. Leaning then on the wall, you gaze out over the landscape, letting it invade you, from your eyes to your imagination to your memory, where something inside, you don't know what, an image come from you can't say where or how, seems to have prepared you for this deep sympathy, this intimate knowledge awakened in you by the view.

In what you see, it's true, there's a lot that is and always was yours, by birth: your country's religious and sensual essence is here; the pooled calm of things is the same; the land, tilled the same way, is spread out in the same iridescent segments; the workers' bodies dotting it here and there, each with its unique dignity, are barely a shade darker than many of your own people's, maybe a bit more mysterious, with a mystery that begs to be penetrated.

But along with all this there's something else, something exotic subtly allied with everything that's yours, that you seem to sense taking possession of you. This is how it must have taken possession of the old conquistadors, with the same inward dominion, as if they had been then, as you are now, the subjugated ones. Something distinct from your Mediterranean, Atlantic world, that emerges here on the other side of this continent, on the other ocean facing a distant Asia, and how perfectly it's matched with you and what's yours, as if your existence only now might finally be complete.

THE IMAGE

The mountain of flowers on the silver stands from one side of the nave to the other nearly dizzies you with its scent combined with that of the incense rising toward the vault, like the flames of the candles burning before the altar in tight rows. Directly opposite, in rows no less dense, the faithful, mostly men, some kneeling, some on their feet, fix their eyes on the image that seems also to have captivated the many children with them.

Years, long years in puritan countries had left you unaccustomed to a faith so absolute before its symbols, of which neither the timid expression of trust with which you see them touch the glass protecting a relic, and then fold their hand back against their body to convey some virtue, nor the lostness of their gaze in adoration seems a sufficient index. But there it is, alive in those bodies, the most enduring work of your race, among these souls who so resemble yours.

The path that led here hardly matters, nor the ancestral ramifications that have come to this: distant gods gone, a cruel cult extinguished. The belief in the supernatural is the same as your own people's; the contemplative attitude also. And in them your thirsty body is refreshed, as in a spring bubbling suddenly out of the ground where it was hidden, though a large part of you could never share the fervor of these creatures, yet close to them you're nearly one with them.

Outside, the big festive sun-drenched plaza, with its countless booths and stands selling flowers and candles, is crowded with people in no particular hurry: graceful movements, soft voices, eloquent glances. Their lives breathe with the certainty of being part of a whole and at the same time free within it; alive through the life of that God of which the visible symbol is there inside, in the basilica, and which can help them and intercede for them, and whose wisdom knows better than human beings what it is that suits them.

THE PEOPLE

These people, these taciturn Indians, in their poverty, in their abandonment, are they as luckless as your human remorse and compassion make them out to be? Faced with them, as with another people of another distant place, your own, your sympathy is elicited. And why this instinctive sympathy of yours toward the common people? Or more precisely: toward what's unique in each of them, more than toward their democratic mass.

The surroundings you grew up in, provincial middle class, had among its more or less groundless pretensions that of feeling different from the common folk, maybe not so much superior as purely and simply different. Later, as you grew up and left those familiar surroundings, their customs, manners, and native and acquired preferences, that initial sense of difference didn't diminish, it increased. But that insistent feeling of difference couldn't obscure the perception of a certain something in common between you and the people.

Because at the end of the day, just like the people, you didn't have much. If by your native circumstances you had certain privileges, you also had certain debts. But the privileges were imaginary and the debts real; that is, without knowing ease or comfort you knew their demands. At times you were grateful for your lot, believing as you do that abundance degrades. Poverty can engender brutality, but wealth stupidity; and one gives way to the other. So might there be in your sympathy toward the people, beneath the artificial sense of difference, a real affinity? Between the people and you, make no mistake, you perceive a space that's difficult to bridge.

Difficult, except by sympathy. And so, where does it come from? What directs it? Because it isn't just compassion. When you wish them better luck, you also know that people, when their luck improves, can lose what nobility they had; now they're just another middle class, but worse, without those aspirations, maybe ridiculous, dictated by an obsolete ideal that can't be improvised. And then?

What connects you with the people is the animal in you: the body, the overwhelming element in life, which even now exerts such power over you, and on account of which you've often felt, not just equal, but inferior to the people. Because the spirit, except insofar as the body can bring it along (and in you it can, and then some), scarcely has a role to play. In you, when the body, the Titanic part, speaks, your spirit, the Dionysian part, if it doesn't surrender, the most it can do is be silent.

Truth is that poetry is also written with the body.

WASTING TIME

The plaza, you have to admit, is ugly; the fountain, you have to admit, absurd. But the night, the air, the trees are kind and incline your spirit to kindness. So that, sitting on a bench, you pass the time, though not that much is left. A laziness, caught from the heat, the darkness, the bodies strolling past, invades you and encounters no resistance.

Nearby are two young guys; one seated, like you, but reading or pretending to read a newspaper; the other lying down, his head at rest in his companion's lap. The reader, whose unbuttoned shirt hangs from his back, sets down the paper to stretch, caressing his naked torso. The sleeping one keeps on sleeping or pretends to keep on sleeping.

The breeze of the tropical night rests on your skin, refreshing it. You feel yourself floating, light, insubstantial. Your senses alone are alert, and with them your body; but it's a relaxed alertness, without the usual intrusions desiring and demanding. And while you, who've known that body forever, may be a bit suspicious of its calm, it claims that one kiss tonight would be enough to make it happy.

UNUSUAL SUNSET

The tiny village is over there, behind the palm trees lining the beach. Under the sunshade, sitting in the hammock, even though it isn't comfortable, sipping the juice from a coconut, even though it isn't cold, laughing at yourself, you take a look at how the day is ending.

Laughing at how out of place you feel, here where everything is new to you: this sea a shade of turquoise barely turning a grayish white; these creatures with dark bodies and blond hair; this perpetual summer climate.

New? For you the tropics have always been a setting you've desired and foreseen. That's why it seems right to find here a measured calm that your reason wasn't counting on but your instinct was. Because you find measure in all of it, even in what might seem to you most extreme: the sunset.

First there's a layer of iridescent clouds spread out in bands across the sky, and behind that there's another, and behind that another, where in the farthest distance you can glimpse a streak of screaming crimson. It's something like the fanned-out tail of a peacock in its radiant magnificence, where cool and blazing colors balance each other.

But now the peacock's tail has folded, and nothing's left of its wild splendor. Twilight was brief as a sigh. Only the ocean seems to have gathered a little light in its breast, and now releases it in a purplish glow, like the color of lead-wort flowers, its surface smooth except for the crashing violence of the waves.

THE CHURCHES

Wherever you go in this country, a church is never far off. On city streets, on country lanes, all of a sudden you see it, announcing its presence with two matching towers, and behind them the dome, like a big coach pulled by a pair of rearing horses. The façade is so tall that it's often difficult to take it all in, up close, as it presents itself at the end of a tree-lined avenue, and even more so if it appears at a distance, with nothing else to put it in perspective.

Yet the conventions of the genus don't rule out a variety of species, since it's rare to see two churches truly alike. What distinguishes them are the incidentals: the color of the stone, the ornamentation bedecking the front. From a simple façade, with scarcely a single decorative motif (imported, but sometimes with Indian traces), to an elaborate one, to whose intricately carved surface not a curlicue or spiral could be added, they span the full range of styles.

It's hard to say whether the native character finds fullest expression, as strangers believe, in the most embroidered kind. Because it's also possible to see the contradiction between that tendency and the composed expression and reserved demeanor common to these people. Unless that luxuriant decoration can be seen, not as a whole thing sought for its own sake, but as an indirect result of a fascination with detail. Whoever tries to get at the truth discovers that one extreme is just as likely as the other, and furthermore that both can be mixed together.

It appears as if the indigenous art, which before had found expression in forms of extreme simplicity and colossal proportions, on receiving the baroque style from outside broke out into all sorts of repressed complications and convolutions. There's no doubt that they go with the surroundings and adapt to them, sometimes in unexpected or ironic ways. Remember that mandolin-playing angel, out of whose head some feathers sprang that seemed to have escaped from his molting wings? Or that ascetic saint cowering in his niche as if in flight from posthumous temptation, while around him circled all the lascivious curves he'd fled from in life?

The ornamentation can be so showy that the nave or the façade becomes a kind of theater and calls for actors. Didn't this happen in the sacristy in Taxco? The paintings, covering the length of the walls with figures, the hammered and burnished moldings of its roof and cornices, the huge gold-plated extravagance of chests and tables, turned it into a perfect set for a speech in one of Calderón's plays or the arias in a Gluck opera. (And also, what a sacrilegious *boudoir*.) It's true that now few churches here are more than an empty shell: the same impulse that raised them ruins them. A shame? Who knows. Someone—was it Heraclitus?—said: "The same road goes both up and down."

DOING NOTHING

Sitting on this veranda, whose vaulted roof gives the appearance of a cloister, past the sloping garden, past the road that borders it, you gaze at the bay. It's early in the morning, and not yet hot. Outside, over one of the arches, hangs a slender branch dripping with scarlet flowers, which obscures the horizon and at the same time, like a thin curtain, lets light through. What kind of tree is that? It's a tropical tree you've never seen before. (Remember to ask what it's called.)

The sound of distant voices makes you look below: with slow movements, dark naked torsos, white pants, straw hats, some men are working on the road. Working? Here your consciousness suddenly seems to be startled. Work? In these surroundings everything is, or seems to be, so gratuitous that the idea of work is out of the question. Let's see. You got here yesterday and you're leaving tomorrow. Is it worth the effort to go over again this forgetfulness of yours about working and your instinctive shock at remembering it?

Let's see. The world of the senses, the sea, the sun, where you think you're living for a few hours—is it real? Isn't it an unfinished dream from your youth, which you keep on pursuing your whole life long? And even if that world were real, would it be truly your own? It's good to make love, to swim, to lie in the sun, but could you live like this for the rest of your life? I know what you're going to say: that world, real or unreal, is plenty. For you, doing nothing is activity enough.

This climate, among other benefits, provides even further evidence of how much vanity and boredom contribute to excessive human activity. To live, does one really have to work so hard? If man were only capable of sitting still in his room for fifteen minutes. But no: he has to do this, and that, and that other thing, and something else besides. Meanwhile, who takes on the task of living? Of living for its own sake? Of living for the pleasure of being alive, and nothing more? Fine. Drop the soliloquy and take a look around.

To look. To look. Is that idleness? Who really looks at the world? Who looks at it with an impartial gaze? Maybe the poet, and no one else. Elsewhere you've said that poetry is the word. And the gaze? Isn't the gaze poetry? Nature likes to hide, and you have to surprise her, with a steady, passionate gaze. The gaze is one wing, the word the other wing of the impossible bird. The poet is made of the gaze and the word, at least. So this is the work that is your idleness: the task of looking and then the task of waiting for the words to arrive.

Now get up and stroll down to the beach. For one morning you've worked about hard enough at doing nothing.

DEATH'S TOYS

These little figures in the museum cases, are they anything more than toys? When you were young some people used to claim, as a way of starting an argument, that art was just a game. You won't say they were right, because they didn't really know what they were talking about. But it could be true that art *is* a game whose dramatic significance they never imagined.

These figures are, or could be, toys, like the Greek and Egyptian ones you've seen displayed in other museums. The artists (or rather craftsmen; let's not get too lofty, enough with pretension) conceived them with no less grace, and their fingers fashioned them with no less skill. Look at that one: a chunky hunchback, naked except for his hood and walking stick, going down the road.

Couldn't it be an image of Titlacaoan the trickster, in one of his various transformations? Like that totally naked woman selling green chiles in the Tulla market, where you can detect the gaze and desire of the handsome daughter of Vemac, the Toltec chieftan? Because in not a few of these figures there is, as in some of the mythic episodes where Titlacaoan appears, a trick being played, a prank, perhaps a bit odd for this people's austere and serious imagination.

Next to these delightful trifles are other figures whose charm is less elusive, and in which it's clearer how much of the dramatic there is in the so-called game of art. Look at that muscular torso, naked, adorned with an enormous necklace and wrapped in a sash. Found in tombs, many of these fragments survived, evading death's interdiction. But what a shame. Here too, as in so many museums, the sheer numbers splinter one's attention.

And yet all this is no cause for lament, since maybe that survival of the fragile and the graceful, when what seemed most resistant to time has vanished, can only be a paradox that might teach our pedantic certainty a lesson. Doesn't death, in giving back these charming knickknacks through the cracks in the door it's hidden behind, like a little delinquent thumbing his nose, seem to be laughing at us?

EYES AND THE VOICE

Whatever a man is, if he's anything, is revealed in his eyes and his voice; so much so, that they can win over whoever sees or hears them. Even a beautiful body, however beautiful it is, needs something more: a spark of light, an echo of music. To lose oneself in a voice, to be consumed by a gaze! Who hasn't wanted that at one time or another?

*

For many years you lived among people with dull voices and expressionless eyes. And it's not because they weren't good people; but their eyes, at best, were stagnant pools, and at worst black holes. Was there anything inside? If so, and you often doubted it, it had died.

And their voices, either angry or indifferent; at both extremes, just noise, noise, noise. Toneless. Those voices were uncultured (culture: legacy of generous voices), unmodulated, insensitive; voices for business or necessity, nothing more.

*

Here, few if any voices are uncultured; however humble the speaker, he speaks a gentle language. A speech that's precise, a classical idiom, free of vulgar slang and boorish attitudes. And how these voices sound, so clear and delicate, like the cool and airy murmur of rustling silk.

These brown eyes, with their lingering gaze that feels and penetrates; eyes where the soul is revealed, that are themselves the soul. In passing, unexpectedly, they fix on one like a blazing sunset, leaving an inchoate pleasure in whoever sees them, and with it the desire to see them again tomorrow.

*

There are those who fall madly in love with greed and those who fall for vanity; those who fall for ambition and those who fall for not wanting to fall for anything; there are those who fall in love with a creature, and you would fall for a pair of eyes and a voice. You'd follow them all the way to hell (if you're not on the way already) for a single word, for a single look, and to you the cost would hardly even matter.

THE MAGIC GROTTO

The nave is like that of any other church here, so many
beautiful ones. But as you cross it, behind a lateral partition,
you find yourself in an unexpected and extraordinary place.
Find yourself? Wouldn't it be more true to say you lose
yourself? Because you *are* lost; reality's been suspended and
you're floating into another medium. What is it? It
emanates from the lamp, there in the vault, as in a deep
well turned upside down in whose depths can be seen, not
the reflection of light, but light itself, which doesn't relieve
the shadows below, and the diffuse clarity seems not to pro-
ceed from the world outside, but to spring, in dazzling
splendor, from this cave itself, from its gold plating.

The walls and ceiling, though it's hardly accurate to
speak of walls and ceiling here, when what surrounds you,
if it resembles anything in this world, is more like the tent
of some barbaric Asiatic warrior, are sunk in a gleaming,
overlaid, nielloed gloom. In the dramatic play of light and
shadow, a wealth of elaborate fauna and flora, wings, claws,
tentacles; trunks, shoots, leaves; thighs, bellies, throats;
long hair, corollas, feathers, everything alive, pulsing and
curving, twisting, turning back on itself, encircling itself,
like forms bubbling up out of chaos. It's a sabbat, a witches'
sabbath, a pandemonium, and only the redundant and
monotonous variation of these words can express, or try to
express, what it is you're seeing.

Calm, a bit of calm, you tell yourself, closing your
eyes. To ask: Do you like it? would be beside the point.
Because we don't ask ourselves if we like a hurricane or a
tornado, and that's how this acts: like an uncontrollable
force of nature, which we endure, just getting through it if

possible, nothing more. And while there's plenty of the primal and elemental in it, isn't there a lot of the artificial as well? Both, the elemental and the artificial, biting each other's tail, mixing together. But the work doesn't even suggest the human; one can't imagine the mind that might have conceived and planned it, nor the hand that designed and shaped it. There is no plan or design, but the confusion of a dream. Nor can memory clarify it, but rather, contrary to the way impressions normally operate, in the ones provoked here, far from purifying them, remembering only increases the confusion.

And that image in the central alcove, rising up in the air, what's it doing here? Are devotion and self-communion possible here? Are even the traditional beliefs of your country and people possible here? Hasn't the imagery usurped belief, and cult displaced religion? A much more ancient cult, in any case, is the one that appears to persist, despite the visible familiar symbols. Deep underground, you think, in a cave, on whose walls so many petrified excoriations, flaring up out of the dark at times, like the eyes of predators, testify to the passing of semidivine monsters, that once had here, together, altar and lair.

. . . One time, it's not so bad, you tell yourself, recovered now from the encounter. Above all if that one time is so fine, so dramatically fine as this one.

DUET

This dark and slender body, on the threshold of adolescence, barely beyond its childhood, your arms hold sweetly in a strong embrace. Dark within the darkness of the room, betrayed only by contrast with the bedsheets' whiteness, it resembles a bit of shadow, so light and brown it is; a warm shadow, but whose touch cools your limbs and ventilates your thoughts. To your enveloping tenderness it responds with abandon, and you don't tire of caressing and kissing it, feeling more than seeing its face, where the eyes gleam with a spark of mischief and even malice.

How long have you been here? Six o'clock, seven o'clock, eight o'clock. When he finally moves to get up, it's only to fall again laughing into your arms, which understanding the game and giving into it, have let him go. Suddenly, outside the windows of the next room, where the lamp gives off a glow, you hear the daily summer downpour of this last hour of the afternoon falling heavily, and almost at the exact same time a thunderclap, which should have come first, announcing it.

Then into your mind spring some centuries-old lines *(Western wind, when will thou blow / The small rain down can rain? / Christ, if my love were in my arms / And I in my bed again!)*, and faced with this out-of-place literary flashback you can't contain your disgust. Literature? Here? Ashamed of your memory, impertinent in this trance of pure animalism, you want to discard, forget these lines of poetry. Without realizing they've been born in you, this cry of a human being and his identical desire, from the same impulse that created them in the soul of their nameless author, like you, long separated, for interminable days, during winter, from a body like this one that you're kissing and caressing, from the same dark, warm embrace of another shadow of the same desire.

A GARDEN

As you pass through the gate, or even before, from the patio entrance, you already feel that leap, that tremolo in your blood signaling a budding sympathy. Again a corner. In how many places, however strange they were to you, have you not found that corner where you felt alive in your own element? Your own? All right. Say it: in that of your kind, and not so much in terms of nationality, even though a lot of your instinctive affinity has to do with your native land, as of temperament. And this corner is one of the most beautiful you've seen.

No, no—you tell yourself, over your own possible objection: the sudden attraction has nothing to do with the corner you're seeing now, and the others that you can compare it with are only a memory. Even though at first glance, taking in the terraces, the stairways, the arbors of the garden, something brings to mind that other one whose image you carry always deep in your soul. But it's crazy to compare: what exists fully, what's right here, is for that reason unique, and nothing can dislodge it or replace it.

There aren't any flowers, or hardly any, except for that magnificent bougainvillea, a shower of purple spray that cascades the full length of one wall. The trees, though hardy, look tired, aged. On the paths, the ground is uneven. A lot of steps are broken. The fountains, dry. There are gaping holes in the walls, without glass or shutters, opening onto roofless rooms, where grass is growing through the pavers. What desolation. And at the same time, what secret enchantment radiates from all this.

Because the desolation here doesn't suggest abandonment. On the contrary, everything indicates careful hands that tend it, that repair as well as possible, with scarce resources, the violations of time. And that's the source of this garden's peculiar charm, like that of a beautiful body, where one can sense a will that's trying, if not to fight off time, to calm, to slow it down. If ever the notion of over-ripeness has seemed to you less sad, it's here: in this place the past, which pervades everything, doesn't diminish its grace but gives it depth, fills it with tranquility.

Past and present are reconciled, are confused, insidiously, to recreate a time already lived, and not by you, a time where, as you pass beneath these branches, you enter, you breathe, you move, a bit ineptly, like someone distracted who lets his feet fall in the same tracks as someone else who preceded him on the same path. Sitting at the edge of the pond, under the arches, you feel to be yours a story that wasn't yours.

This breeze stirring the branches is the same air that rustled through them before, on another day, at this same hour. This nostalgia isn't yours, but someone's who felt it years ago in this same spot. This expectation isn't yours, but someone else's who waited here one evening for his lover. And so, abandoned to the lethal influence of the place, all of a sudden you're overtaken by fear, by the attraction of living, desiring, atoning for the actions of someone now dead, of being lost forever, like a phantom, in a confluence of time.

THE MARKET

Eastward, on the road to the ocean, you passed by a market day in that village. In the plaza, beneath the branches, among various vendors, some displaying their merchandise on stands and other, poorer ones spreading out their goods on the ground, men and women were filing past. Filing? Mostly in still groups that were also quiet, the scene appeared to you less like real life than a painting of a crowd. It wasn't only its stillness that made you see it as a play of illusory appearances, but the arranged marvel of its postures and costumes.

The women, wrapped in their dark rebozos, black, blue or brown, above which shone the darkness of their parted hair, and below, the ocher of their naked feet. The men, in white or pink or cream or sky-blue shirts and pants, over their shoulders those graceful ponchos that go by the even more graceful name, jorongo, against whose muted background bright tones flashed. The same as occurs in certain birds, while the neutral plumage of the female scarcely stood out, it was the male who gratuitously displayed his colors and ornamentation.

Who was buying? Who was selling? Under the overcast light of the morning, this scene, its voices low, its gestures reserved, appeared to you to have no other motive than to compose for visual contemplation a purely esthetic image. As in the canvas of some classical Sevillean painter, the air was the only actor; actor, and at the same time the subtle artisan, coloring and shaping everything you saw with that magical touch, unknown to northern reality and painting, whose strength is also delicate and its grace, severe.

Feeling yourself an intruder, yet longing not to abandon such a place, you approached one of those figures to ask a question. But it was a pretext; a pretext to enter, to place yourself subtly in the picture with her. Like a separate figure, just barely visible at the edge and in the background of the canvas, seen in a mirror, you stood there, elusive actor and invisible witness, reflected in someone's eyes.

PROPERTY

"I," said Albanio finally, "have no desire to own property. Property, who can account for its malicious influence? It doesn't belong to us, we belong to it; it's the possessor and we're the possessed."

"No, no, no, no, no, no," Abelardo, Poncio, Arístedes, Sofronio, Nuño and Testifonte all interrupted at the same time. Cardenio, who didn't care, and Fidel, who was shy, said nothing.

"Yes, my friends. You're prisoners of your property and to your property you're not even men, but objects. That dignified, self-sufficient expression of yours, which you didn't have when young, because then a person is just what he is, not what he owns, is it anything more than a mask concealing your real face, if it still exists, that your property makes you wear to prove you love it? If you could at least own it as if it wasn't yours! I think some mystic should have said that before. Then there might still be some hope for you."

"You're attacking property?" exclaimed Testifonte. "If your parents hadn't respected it, and collected it, what kind of paradox would you be talking about now?"

"I'm not attacking anything," said Albanio, "much less property; your property, my property, eh! I know full well we're all in a blind alley. It was just a matter of amusing ourselves for a while."

Just then Choco sneezed. They'd forgotten he was there.

Like a house pet who knows where the warmth and sympathy are, he was next to Albanio, seated on the floor. Though he said nothing, skilled as he was in silence and with such an expressive face, his silence was eloquent enough for those who knew how to look at him.

"Don't tell me your protégé would come to see you so often if you didn't own property," Testifonio insisted.

"Look at him," said Albanio, placing his hand on Choco's shoulder. "He's so stripped clean of everything, of everything that's not his body and his soul, he couldn't be any more naked. Because he has nothing, not even parents. Where does he eat? Where does he sleep? Does he really even eat or sleep? The only thing he possesses, and it doesn't possess him but *is* him, is his grace; and he'll lose even this, once he's a grown man. But that doesn't mean he'll cease to be himself, the way we've stopped being what we were. Because his soul will stay whole, and that will sustain him.

"I don't know what I envy more, his youth, his grace, or his poverty. Can one even talk about poverty in this case? His poverty makes me horrified of my property. When we love someone, we want to be like that person, we want to be that person. Ah, to have nothing, as if that meant having everything! That's his freedom.

"You think he really wants the little money I can give him? Isn't his acceptance of it a game, a diversion he lends himself to, knowing that money is just the ticket, the passport to being here with us, even sitting on the floor, at our feet, the way he is? Or isn't it just out of courtesy (these people are so terribly courteous) that he takes it, knowing that faith in money is our religion and that's all we've got?

"Don't tell me I'm wrong," he said to deflect whatever objection the others might raise. "I don't want to be wrong about this too; I don't want to be wrong about this, at least."

Was Choco, his face impassive, his body motionless, like a little dark idol, listening to Albanio? Not even Choco himself could be sure.

THE PATIO

It's midafternoon, and as you leave this gallery of the convent, through the white arches, with its fountain in the center surrounded by orange trees, you see the patio. Half courtly, half rustic, it's flooded with sun and calm; calm filtered through the centuries, life soothed. Sitting on one of the stone benches, you look, drinking it in, with the pleasure of one deprived a long time of some good, and finding it at last, and still incredulous, possessing it.

In a faraway land, across the seas, here you find traced, with rock and tree and water, a little corner of what's yours, a little Andalusian corner. The soft, lazy breeze bathing your soul, isn't it that same air, doesn't it come from over there? Yet the intrusion of a distant atmosphere, in the midst of the present, doesn't suggest obliviousness or disdain of it, but rather a rare coincidence and affinity.

Seeing this corner, breathing this air, you find that what you're looking at and breathing is also inside you; that there in the depths of your soul, in its dark circle, like the moon reflected in deep water, is the exact image of what's surrounding you: and ever since your childhood it rises, full and clear, that essential image, sustaining with its lightness the weight of your life and its secret longing.

That's how the man you are knows who he is, by embracing now the boy he was, and the singular existence they share has its roots in a secret and silent corner of the world. You understand then that if this other half of life is still alive, maybe you're doing nothing but recovering finally, in the present, your lost childhood, when the boy, by a gift of grace, was master of what the grown man later, after not a few waverings, mistakes and wrong turns, has to reclaim by force.

DAYBREAK IN THE GULF

At dawn, the beach deserted and still asleep, you're already in the water. The reddish air and whitish sea, both warm even this early, almost don't cool you off, although they brace your poorly rested, hot-blooded body. Animal well-being gladdens your soul.

Down the beach, at a distance, the cantina's sunshade is all you can see, its tables and benches safely in shadow. Behind it, stands of palm trees, less decoration than proof of latitude. Hot land.

The sun comes up, and still no one. This is the world: sun, sand, water. Solitude and time reside here, nothing else. You? You are just its incidental thought, child of that discovered solitude and that slowed time. A pause.

To live always this way. So that nothing, neither dawn nor beach nor solitude were transit toward some other time, some other place, some other person. Death? No. Life sustained, with a here and a there, but without regrets or desires.

And between before and after, like the pearl between its valves, this perfect shimmering instant. Now.

POSSESSION

The body doesn't want to disappear without first having been consumed. And how is a body consumed? The mind doesn't quite know how to describe it, even though it conceives more clearly this ambition of the body's, which the body only glimpses. The body knows only that it's isolated, terribly isolated, while before it, united, whole, creation is calling it.

The world's forms, perceived by the body through its senses, with the deep attraction they provoke (colors, sounds, smells), awaken in the body an instinct that it too is part of this admirable sensual world, but that it's separate from and outside of it, not in it. To enter that world, of which it is an isolated part, to fuse with it!

But the body lacks the spirit's means to fuse with the world; the spirit can possess it all without possessing it, or as if it didn't possess it. The body can only possess things, and even then only for a moment, through contact with them. That's how, when they've left their trace on it, the body knows things.

It's not the body's fault: being what it is, it has to do what it does, it has to want what it wants. Master it? Dominate it? Easy enough to say. The body warns us that we're it for just a brief time, and it too must be made real in its way, and it needs our help to do this. Poor body, innocent animal so cruelly slandered; its impulses seen as beastly, though beastiality is of the spirit.

That land was before you, and you were defenseless before it. Its attraction was precisely the kind your nature needed: everything in it fit your desire. An instinct to fuse with it, to be absorbed in it, pressed on your being, all the more so when the precarious glimpse was offered for just an instant. And how could a body be made to subsist on immaterial memories?

It was in an embrace that you felt your being fused with that land; through a smooth dark body, dark as a shadow, smooth as fruit, you achieved oneness with the land that had created it. And you could forget everything, everything but that touch of your hand on a body, a memory that seems to throb, deeply, secretly, with the very pulse of life.

THE INDIAN

At times with his children, at others alone; selling something that appears not to matter to him, or without any pretext at all for his motionless presence; barefoot and squatting in the dust, big straw hat tipped over his eyes, where you might just barely be able to guess what he's feeling or thinking; look at him.

The slavemasters fell. The conquerors were conquered in their turn. Revolutions fought and forgotten. Only he keeps on being what he was; true to himself, he can let the appearances of time fall like a curtain over the superficial turmoil of the world.

He's the man that other peoples call uncivilized. How much they could learn from him. There he is. He's more than a man: he's a decision facing the world. Better? Worse? Who knows. You, at least, admit that you don't know. But deep in your heart you understand him.

Look at him, you who believed yourself a poet, and know now where all works, beliefs, ambitions end. For him, who owns nothing, desires nothing, something deeper sustains him; something centuries old that he still stands for. It's a shame that chance didn't bring you into the world among his kind.

It would be too much to ask him to ignore his poverty, to forget misfortune, to submit to death. But thank you, Lord, for creating and saving him; thank you for letting us still see someone for whom Your world is not a mad bazaar or a senseless carnival.

A MAN'S CENTER

You've lived many years with your body in one place, your soul in another; while necessity tied you to one side, pleasure and affection pulled you toward the other. Optimists, pretending that the best place to find themselves is the situation they're in, forget that the spirit, just like the body, can't live in hostile—or more precisely, alien—surroundings. Somehow it will catch (from whom?) the disease.

No, he's not an angel nor a devil-in-exile. What you're speaking of here is a man, nothing more; on earth, nothing more. The two, man and earth, if they can find the harmony between them, are enough. And don't even try to pretend your life is one of the few that's lacking this harmony, because you know full well, and that's why you can speak of it, that this is an illness many suffer, and you're just one among them.

For a few days you found your center in that land, because souls in their way also have their center on earth. The feeling of being a stranger, which in the past pursued you wherever you were living, fell silent there and finally went to sleep. You were in your own place, or in a place that felt like your own; you felt attuned to everything, or nearly everything, and things, air, light, landscape, people, were your friends. As if a gravestone had been lifted off of you, you lived as if brought back to life.

When, on the return flight, at dawn, you saw the sky and the earth of the North, with those others so different still present in your imagination and whom to your sorrow you were leaving behind, you had to hide the tears in your eyes. Once more you kept your feelings to yourself (who else but you would have any use for your feelings?), giving the seemingly correct impression to those who still accuse you of being cold and incapable of love.

EMPTY SHELL

This tune, this song you unconsciously find yourself humming under your breath, is something you heard there and unconsciously learned there. But now, as you hum it to yourself, it's changed, and it isn't just the song that comes along with it, but the very reality of those days when you learned it. Before you is that window, in your hotel room; the crown of that palm tree rising out of a little garden; the profile of those terraces, against a sky with a few white clouds adrift in it. And what you see, like the stone inside a fruit, is surrounded by that city, that world, of which your room was the center; the scene of that day, always the same, always different, as you grew accustomed to being there, spilling out of yourself, careless, amused, aimlessly wandering, guided by your feeling, your mood of the moment, which was nothing more than a natural response to that setting.

When you heard this tune there not even paying attention, you never thought you'd find in it later, yourself doubly distant, in space and in time, all that just as it was, and with it your summer self; that it would bring back one of the rare moments in your life whose memory isn't bitter. Because this tune encompasses a few weeks of your life, that life of yours is now this song, and every time you hum it you'll see appearing, as you do now, the same sky, the same city, the same surroundings, revived in this trivial, ephemeral tune, which for that very reason can give the appearance of that life of yours which was also trivial and ephemeral, and which, like a spirit in distress seeking a body to return to, has found its incarnation in the empty spiral of the melody.

Poetry, painting, sculpture, other physical forms of art, once remembered, can't give back those moments of your life, because their material being is caught in its own existence, it is its own existence, and offers no space where yours might enter it. Music, on the other hand, made of sound, of the most disembodied thing that exists for us, creatures of flesh and blood, is completely fluid and insubstantial. That's why we can enter it, and invest it with our actions, give it our thoughts, our desires, appropriate it as an expression of our own existence. However lofty or noble it may be, we can still master it, enslave it for our own purposes, impose upon it our human weight of a creature whose existence drifts at the mercy of oblivion.

But if this melody holds and returns to you the outline of those days when it entered your life, of what without it would be an abstraction, a disembodied longing, a desire without an object, a love without a lover, it's also only for a moment, as a mirror holds and returns for a moment the image you've entrusted to it. Because once you've gone, who else could find that trace of what you were, deciphering that echo of yours, those hours, that past you've entrusted it with? Everything will come down with you, like tinsel streamers once the party's over, even the shadow of a few days that lingered a while in music, and no one else will be able to evoke for the world what ends in the world with you.

Pitiful? For you, maybe. But you're nothing more than one more card in the game, and it, though it hurts to acknowledge it, is not played by you or for you, but with you and for an instant.

RETURN

Nearly a year has passed, and again you find yourself in this land. Again your gaze takes in, under the transparency of the air, the ground's severity: a flat plain, whose nakedness isn't covered but accentuated by the nopal, the century plant, the agave. Before you, and in the background, the mountains, which must be scaled. Again you're in a land whose rhythm and accent accord with those of your absent one, with the people close to your heart.

Can't you hear them? One mixed up with the other, don't they seem to sound in your ears behind the echo of that young man's voice you heard singing and strumming a guitar in the customs house as you crossed the border? The thickness of the walls, the height of the ceiling, amplified the volume of his voice, revealing and accentuating, like the blowup of a detail in a photograph unnoticed at first glance, the energy and fragility, the wildness and the culture in the tune.

You almost don't believe your senses. Are you really here? You're not just imagining this? Its memory and its image came with you and sustained you over so many long and worthless and endless months of winter, so tedious and desolate and empty, that you can scarcely believe in its reality. Love is so strange, and how surprisingly it springs up, dragging behind it one's will and one's whole being, with reasons only it is aware of, in a deep and singular impulse.

Yes, here it is, before your eyes, the object of your love: look at it, you whose gaze has so seldom been graced with the view you've loved. This plain, this sky, this air envelope you and absorb you, annihilating you in them. Now love is not just inside, drowning you in its vastness, but outside, visible and tangible; and you are part of it at last, breathing freely. You think it good to be alive, good to have lived. All your joy, all your fervor revive in your soul the sense of the divine. And you thank God, who has kept you alive to experience this one moment you've desired.

SUMMING UP

"This country grew out of another one that was ruthlessly destroyed. Remember who destroyed it?"

"The same ones who later, carefully and watchfully, tried to revive it in their way: my people."

"Then perhaps what draws you to it is no more than a subtle retrospective kind of national pride. Didn't you think you'd find in this land the same ancestral defects as in your own?"

"The same virtues as well. When I'd almost stopped believing in my land, seeing this one restored my faith in my own, whose defects wouldn't exist without its virtues."

"What virtue could your fallen country have?"

"That of having put the spirit above everything."

"And that's what made it so good."

"Yes. That's what made it so bad."

"Fine. But this other land is not the same as your own, nor are these people. Don't you feel that to them you can only be a stranger? More than a stranger: someone from a country they may still view with disgust?"

"That's all true. But does it matter? If we never did anything in life except what's rational, we'd be lost. We have to use whatever capacity for affection exists in us, without determining beforehand whether or not it makes sense."

"Who asked for your affection here? When human beings have put so much distance between them, affection can't get across."

"It's because the separation exists that the sympathy springing up now can be so deep and sincere."

"Don't you think that sympathy might really be a disguise for a certain atavistic remorse, an inadequate compensation for past debts?"

"Could be. That's why it can and should be so one-sided, without any expectation it will be returned, which love doesn't need in order to exist."

"Nevertheless, admit it . . ."

"What?"

"Your sympathy would have been gratified by a friendly gesture, in response."

"The person called by my name is not the one who's been speaking here."

"An impersonal attitude? Impersonal words?"

"I detest the intrusion of the person into what the poet writes."

"That attitude might have admitted, then, amid your unconditional sympathy, a few objections. There's so much in this country to object to. Didn't you see it?"

"It's easy to see. But maybe that's the condition, at least in part, if not completely, for the existence of what I came in search of: the land and its historic will, which is the people."

"You have a rationalization for everything."

"Love never fails to find them."

"Exactly. Do you think these people are going to understand, let alone accept, your love's rationalizations even when they follow their own logic?"

"I'm telling you, all I wanted was to feel that sympathy. What happens later with the gift of that sympathy doesn't concern me. Like a child at play in a game of his own invention, with that same unconditional involvement, I've launched my paper boat, which in any event is bound to be lost on the current."

Coda

WRITTEN IN WATER

Ever since childhood, as far back as I can remember, I've always sought what doesn't change, I've longed for eternity. Everything around me contributed, in my early years, to sustaining in me the illusion and the belief in what lasts: the unchanging family home, the identifying accidents of my life. If anything changed, it was only to return later to its usual state, everything proceeding like the year's cycle of seasons, and behind the apparent change an intimate unity always shone through.

But childhood ended and I tumbled into the world. People around me died and houses fell into ruin. As I was then possessed by the delirium of love, I didn't pay any attention to this evidence of human decay. If I had discovered eternity's secret, if I possessed eternity in spirit, what did the rest matter? But no sooner had I pressed a body close to mine, believing my desire was imbuing it with permanence, than it fled my arms leaving them desolate.

Later I loved animals, trees (I've loved a black poplar, a white poplar), the earth. Everything disappeared, planting in my solitude the bitter feeling of the ephemeral. I alone seemed to last amid the transience of things. And then, cruelly certain, the notion of my own disappearance dawned in me, the sense that I too one day would abandon my self.

God, I said then, give me eternity! God for me was still the love not attainable in this world, the love forever unbroken, triumphant over the double-edged trick of time and death. And I loved God like the perfect and incomparable friend.

It was just another dream, because God does not exist. The dry leaf, crushed in passing, told me so. The dead bird told me, its broken wing rotting on the ground. Consciousness told me, knowing it too will be lost one day in the vastness of nonbeing. And if God doesn't exist, how could I? I don't exist even now, dragging myself like a shadow through a delirium of shadows, breathing these breathless words, absurd testimony (by whom and for whom?) of my existence.

A NOTE ON THE AUTHOR

Luis Cernuda, one of Spain's leading twentieth-century poets, was born in Seville in 1902 and came of age amid the stellar literary cohort known as the Generation of 1927. The first edition of his collected poems, *La realidad y el deseo*, was published to broad acclaim in 1936 on the eve of the Spanish Civil War. Within two years Cernuda had left Spain permanently, first to teach in England and Scotland, and then in the United States, before finally settling in Mexico, where he died in 1963. Regarded by many Spanish poets and critics as the most influential poet of his generation, Cernuda up to now is less well-known in the U.S. than some of his contemporaries. His *Selected Poems* appeared in English in 1977. *Written in Water* is the first English translation of his prose poems.

A NOTE ON THE TRANSLATOR

Stephen Kessler is a poet, prose writer and translator whose versions of Vicente Aleixandre, Jorge Luis Borges, Julio Cortázar, Pablo Neruda, César Vallejo and other Spanish and Latin American writers have been widely praised. His recent books of original poetry include *After Modigliani* and *Tell It to the Rabbis*. He is a contributing editor of *Poetry Flash* and the editor of *The Redwood Coast Review*.